Moonlit Mayhem

Quantrill's Raid of Olathe, Kansas

Jonathan A Jones

FLOATING SPARK PUBLISHING

Moonlit Mayhem: Quantrill's Raid of Olathe, Kansas
2020 Edition
©2021 Jonathan Jones, All Rights Reserved
Printed and bound in the United States of American

For information contact Floating Spark Publishing
1660 N Hunter Dr
Olathe, KS 66061
www.JonathanJonesAuthor.com

admin@JonathanJonesAuthor.com

Available in these formats:
ISBN: 978-1-7364633-0-7 (Paperback)
ISBN: 978-1-7364633-1-4 (Kindle)
ISBN: 978-1-7364633-2-1 (E-Book)

Library of Congress Control Number: 2021900995

This book is dedicated to my father, Charles Jones Jr., who always believed that I could accomplish anything, regardless of how unlikely I knew that success might be.

Acknowledgements

Jill Jones
Jennifer Healy, Editor
Polly Blair, Editor

Advanced Readers
Steve Hitchcock
Matt Brown
Jeff Jones
Charles Blair
Robert Courtney

Emory Cantey http://www.canteymyerscollection.com/

Staff at RTA Olathe
Kansas State Archives
Kansas State Historical Society
Olathe Historical Society

Table of Contents

Preface

I have been interested in the American Civil War my entire life. My wife, Jill, and I have traveled extensively, and she has grudgingly agreed to visit more battlefields and other Civil War sites than she ever dreamed she would see before our marriage. I was born and raised in Harrisonville, Missouri, which is in the heart of the Border War territory. As a child, the view that Missouri was good, and Kansas was evil was instilled in me by family, friends and neighbors. This "hatred" of Kansas was "playful" in my childhood and certainly did not rise to the level which existed during the 1800s.

In my formative years, many of us had friends or family that lived in Kansas and we frequently went over to "the dark side" to buy beer, (you only had to be 18 to buy beer in Kansas, in Missouri the age was 21) eat at restaurants and go shopping at Oak Park Mall. Athletic contests between the University of Missouri and the University of Kansas were always circled on the calendar and filled with venom and extra importance on both sides. The Missouri vs Kansas games were dubbed and marketed as "The Border War", paying homage to the historical problems between the two states. I was raised to "dislike" Kansas and I didn't really know why. None of my friends knew the reasons either, but this was how many of our parents were raised, and their parents were raised, etc. I'm sure the reverse was true for children raised on the Kansas side.

Fast forward thirty years to 2019 when my wife and I were looking to move back to the Kansas City area. Our three children were grown so we were not worried about school districts and we were willing to live anywhere if we found a house and neighborhood we liked. We had no intention of moving to Kansas. We were Missourians; however, we thought that we should at least keep our options open just in case the perfect house came available on the "dark side" of the state line. Of course, the perfect house ended up being in Olathe, Kansas. When we did our final pros and cons list to decide whether to purchase the house in Olathe, the cons included: "it's in Kansas". There was no logical reason for this feeling, only that we were both "Missourians" and would rather not live in Kansas. Ignoring the good-natured opinions of family and friends, we decided to purchase the Olathe house. We were moving to the "dark side".

At the time of our move, I was working on some family history to add to the research that my grandmother had done many years before. She had been born in Olathe, as had my father, which was something I discovered during my research. This search led me to many interesting Kansas connections. One of those connections is mentioned in the book as it pertains to Quantrill's raid on Olathe. These connections piqued my interest and I started looking into different aspects of my family's history in Kansas. Through this research, I landed on Quantrill's raid of Olathe as a possible topic for a book, something that had always been on my bucket list.

I have done my best to present a balanced view of the time period. Due to very biased newspapers of the time, a researcher must read between the lines and sometimes balance the reported facts from each side to arrive at the truth. The primary sources from the Civil War era, and in fact, for many years after, tended to be extremely biased. While the historical records have landed closer to the truth in the years since the war ended, I have found sources where the views of the writer obviously lie either with the Confederacy or with the Union. As late as 1980, one Missouri writer depicts the Border War this way, "The Missourians had invaded Kansas for a political end. The Kansans came to Missouri for plunder, and to settle the score. The Missourians had been led by their old nobility. The Kansas leaders were upstarts – all-to-often [sic] human dregs brought to the top by turmoil" (Brophy 15). My research would eventually tell me that the Kansas viewpoint was exactly the opposite to that of the Missouri writer.

The Border War on the Missouri and Kansas border is a large and complex topic. The purpose of this work is not to go into detail on every aspect and event of that conflict. Rather, this work focuses on the Raid of Olathe. The chapters before and after the story of the raid are meant to provide a high-level background and a summary of what happened before and after that event. Additional resources for the topics in the book are listed in the bibliography section. I encourage readers to go further to learn more about this period and the absolute hell that it must have been for the residents to live in this time on the border of Missouri and Kansas. I have also included modern maps and images that show the reader exactly where some of these events took place in the context of what is there today. I encourage readers to take a drive through Olathe and imagine what took place at these locations in 1862. Enjoy.

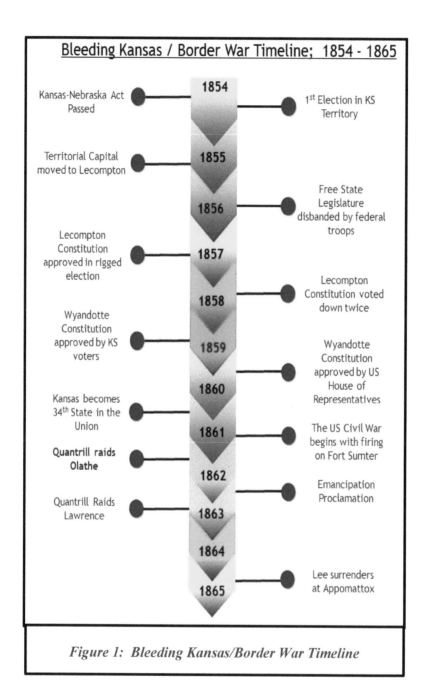

Figure 1: Bleeding Kansas/Border War Timeline

Life in Kansas: 1854-1860

In 1853, most of the occupants of the Kansas Territory were Native Americans. The US Government was negotiating with most of these tribes to move them out of the territory. They felt that the Kansas Territory was going to be important in the future as a highway to the goldfields of the west as well as a potential route for the establishment of the transcontinental railroads. By 1854, most of these tribes had been "relocated" to areas outside of the Kansas Territory. The Kansas Territory was officially opened for white settlers with the passage of the Kansas-Nebraska Act on May 30, 1854.

Most of the settlers that came to the new Kansas Territory did not come for political purposes, they came for land and opportunity. That said, there certainly were political groups who sponsored settlers to come to Kansas and ensure that Kansas was settled with their particular political viewpoint. At the time, the political question was whether Kansas would be a free-state or a slave state. The New England Emigrant Aid Society was an abolitionist group from the east coast that promoted their cause and paid for settlers to move from that area to the Kansas Territory with the aim of making sure that the territory was populated with people who were against slavery. The first group of 29 male settlers arrived in August of 1854 and settled the town of Lawrence, which would always be known as the center for abolitionist activity.

The pro-slavery side of the issue also sent people to Kansas to try and impose their political views. While this group did not have an organized movement to fund and settle the newly opened territory, they did have the advantage of having supporters "right next door" in Missouri, a predominantly pro-slavery state. This made it easier for them to send pioneers and create new settlements in the new territory. David Rice Atchison, a senator from Platte City, Missouri, called for Missourians to, "...resist the abolitionist plot to surround their state with free territory." Atchison led the effort to get Missourians into Kansas and helped establish the pro-slavery cities of Atchison and Leavenworth. (Immigration)

The New England Emigrant Aid Society got a great deal of press and

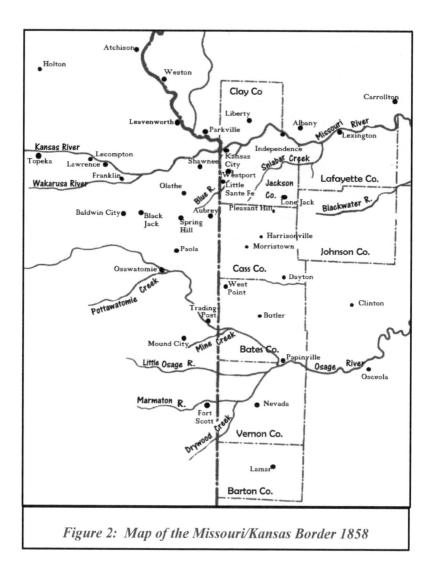

Figure 2: Map of the Missouri/Kansas Border 1858

continues to be credited today with sending large numbers of settlers to Kansas. The reality was that most of the settlers of Kansas came from the border states, including Missouri. From the chart below you can see the origins of the 1860 population, which at that time totaled 107,209.

It is likely that the New England Emigrant Aid Society, whose efforts only contributed 3.9% of the population, gets so much credit for settling Kansas because the settlers from this group were "noisy" and very much in the forefront of the news of the day regarding the slavery issues in Kansas.

While most of the settlers had an opinion of how Kansas should be settled, a significant portion of them just wanted land and opportunity. They were not going to Kansas for political reasons. Most early settlers

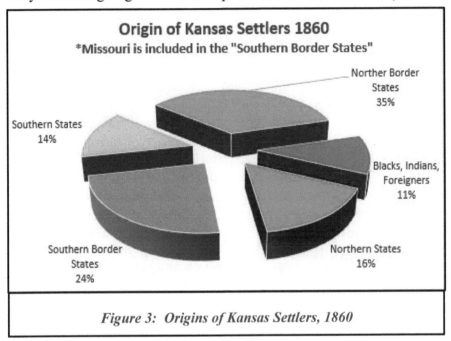

Figure 3: Origins of Kansas Settlers, 1860

probably leaned to one side or the other on the slavery question. That said, the majority of Kansas settlers were not affected personally by the issue and, in truth, likely would have preferred that Kansas be free from "negroes" in general, slave or free. Most of these settlers did not own slaves. It was not plantation owners that came to Kansas. It was farmers, tradesmen and others looking for economic opportunity, who came to settle the new territory. Many of these white settlers felt that slavery was an economic issue rather than a moral or political one. Slavery took jobs away from white settlers. Plantation owners, who owned slaves, could produce more crops which in turn lowered the prices that could be achieved for crops across the region.

A story was told by Senator Jim Lane at an Iowa anti-slavery rally in which he laid out a scenario where a carpenter had been working for a wealthy landowner and had been doing quite well, earning a good living with work from that landowner. One day the landowner purchased two slaves with carpentry skills thus ending the work for the white carpenter. This story exemplified the impact that slavery could have on the common white man (Grim Chieftain 3).

While slavery was the main political issue at the time. It was not the moral side of the institution that was the focus; rather, it was the fact that slavery had a direct correlation to whether the country was going to be controlled by agricultural or industrial concerns. The Republicans were largely made up of northerners who wanted the nation to become an industrial state. The Democrats, on the other hand, were a nationwide party, comprised of both a southern and a northern wing. The northern Democrats had to play nice with their southern brethren as that group held considerable power in the U.S. Senate. This "split" in the Democratic party is what would allow Abraham Lincoln, a Republican, to be elected in 1860. Lincoln took advantage of the Democrat party splitting their votes between their northern and southern factions. The balance of slave states and free states in the U.S. Government was critical to these parties as they both feared that if the scale was tipped one way or the other, the government and laws enacted by that government would tip in that direction also. Until the Kansas-Nebraska Act, which gave the residents of those two new U.S. territories the right to choose whether their state would be slave or free, the U.S. Congress had always taken steps to ensure that the balance between the two sides remained equal each time states were added.

White settlers also felt that if slavery was allowed, the state would be settled by plantation owners who would buy up large tracts of the best land. These large plantations would make it harder for smaller farmers to make a living since the large plantations with a slave workforce could produce much more at lower prices. The fact that slavery was not considered a moral issue is made clear by the contents of the Free-State Topeka Constitution. The initial version of this document, while outlawing slavery, also contained a clause that did not allow free "negroes" to settle in the state. The "no negro" clause would not be included in the final version of the document which was submitted to and rejected by the U.S. Congress.

With all the events happening around Kansas, the practice of slavery never really took hold even though many people were supposedly fighting to make Kansas a slave state. The 1860 census shows only two slaves in Kansas at that time. Prior to 1860, there were likely more slaves than that, but as the 1850s and "Bleeding Kansas" played out, the owning of slaves meant putting a target on your back for the free-state Jayhawker bands that roamed the Kansas countryside.

Another political reason to move to Kansas was to keep Kansas from becoming a home for large amounts of free negroes and runaway slaves. At this time, slaves were considered property and very few white citizens, regardless of their opinions as to whether Kansas should be a free or slave state, wanted them living in their towns or even in a neighboring state. Many pro-slavery Missourians came to Kansas for this reason as well as having a desire to "preserve our way of life". A "way of life" that included owning slaves as property. Many Missourians and Southerners in general had been ingrained since birth that the "Northerners" were trying to tell them how to live and that this must be stopped at all costs. Slavery was certainly an issue for these Southerners, but it was just one of many along with state's rights and northern industrial thinking that would eventually lead to the Civil War.

Life for these early Kansas settlers was physically demanding. Upon their arrival in the territory, their initial priority was to build a safe and functional home for their families. Many men came by themselves intending to send for their families once they were settled. Many of these same men either died in the first few years or gave up and returned east to their families. When a settler and his family arrived at their new homestead in Kansas, they needed to build shelter and find, or create, sources of food and water for their families and livestock. The Kansas weather was brutal. The summers could see temperatures over 100 degrees, and the winter could see temperatures below zero degrees Fahrenheit. This wide range variance in climate, in addition to a drought during 1858-59 made settling in Kansas hard enough without having to worry about the acquisition of supplies or a guerrilla band coming and destroying everything you had built. Remember, Kansas in 1854 was largely devoid of any large settlements. This meant that there were very few stores to purchase supplies, food, seed, clothing, etc. These settlers would often have to rely on trips to Westport, Missouri, or traveling peddlers to get any supplies that they might need. The supplies in these places were also very expensive as low supplies dictated high costs. The securing of supplies was made even more difficult by the Missouri border ruffians who would purposely stop supplies from getting to Kansas if they felt the supplies were meant for free-state settlements, like Lawrence or Olathe.

   The Lane Trail, named after James Lane, was established in 1855 as a route to get free-state settlers and supplies into Kansas that would avoid the pro-slavery Missouri towns.   The trail was marked with stacked stones called "Lane Chimney's" to let travelers know that they

Figure 4: Approximate route of Lane's Trail

were on the right path.   The Lane Trail passed through Iowa and Nebraska to try and get around the Missourians who would attempt to stop the flow of settlers and supplies to towns such as Lawrence and Topeka. By the 1850s, the need for the trail by white settlers was reduced. Instead, the trail began to be heavily used as a route for the underground railroad to get slaves to the north.

   The period between 1854 to 1859, commonly known as the "Bleeding Kansas" era, which will be discussed in detail in the next chapter, made the life of the Kansas settlers even more difficult. Imagine having worked hard to build a farm with a cabin, fences and outbuildings over the course of several months or years only to have a group of men who disagreed with your political views come by and burn it all down, taking anything of value that you had been able to acquire. This was an everyday fear for Kansas settlers and it really didn't matter which side of the slavery issue they supported.

There are striking similarities regarding the divide in the people of the United States in 1855 Kansas when compared to what exists in the country today. The news media of the time was very biased. Most newspapers of the day were either considered pro-slavery or anti-slavery. Many of them even labeled themselves in the name of the paper such as the *Anti-Slavery Bugle* from Lisbon Ohio. Most didn't go this far but were known to be on one side or the other. Olathe had two papers; a free-state paper, The *Olathe Mirror*, and a pro-slavery paper, The *Olathe Herald*. People at this time were often immediately linked to one side or the other by the newspaper they read, their accents, or maybe even simply where they came from. Most towns of any size also had hotels for free-staters and pro-slavery travelers. A traveler took his life in his own hands if he were to choose to stay in the wrong hotel. It was very difficult to be "neutral". Settlers had to pick a side, which turned out to be a real problem, particularly for Missourians along the Kansas/ Missouri border. Order Number 11 enacted by Union General Thomas Ewing, in 1863 made being "neutral" illegal for Missourians living in the border counties by forcing those residents to publicly declare where their loyalties laid. More on Order Number 11 in a future chapter.

Political Events That Triggered the Bleeding Kansas Era

Throughout the first part of the 1800s, the United States government was dominated by the struggle between the northern anti-slavery states and southern pro-slavery states with each side doing whatever they could to ensure that they achieved the voting majority. In 1820, the Missouri Compromise was passed by Congress. This legislation admitted Maine as a free-state and admitted Missouri as a slave state, thus appeasing both sides and maintaining a balance. There was additional language in the bill which added a rule that, except for Missouri, slavery would not be allowed in any new state north of a line drawn at 36° 30' latitude. This imaginary line followed the southern border of Missouri and continued to the west to the ocean.

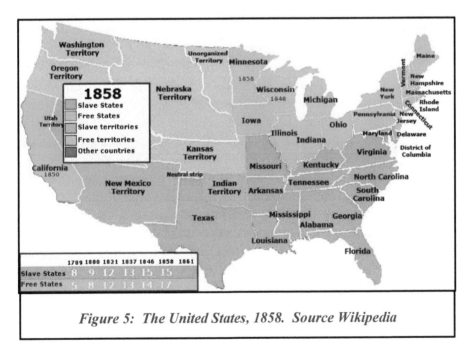

Figure 5: The United States, 1858. Source Wikipedia

The Missouri Compromise put a band-aid on the simmering question of the future of slavery in the United States. With the admission of California as a state under the Compromise of 1850, Congress basically did an end-run around the requirements of the Missouri Compromise. In this act, Congress admitted California to the Union as a Free-State but maintained the balance in the Senate by requiring the new state to have one of their senators to be a pro-slavery supporter.

In 1854, Congress would take this a step further and effectively repeal the Missouri Compromise with the passage of the Kansas-Nebraska Act. The Kansas-Nebraska Act, effective on May 30, 1854, essentially set the wheels for the Civil War in motion. It would begin a dangerous and devastating period in the life of those who lived along the Missouri/Kansas border for the next several years. At this point, the free-staters were gaining political advantage in the United States due to the addition, or expected addition, of the northern states of Iowa and Minnesota. In 1854 the question concerned the admission of Kansas and Nebraska. Pro-slavery proponents were nervous regarding admitting these two states because both were above the Missouri Compromise line. Nebraska, due to its geographic location, was thought to be an obvious free-state. If Congress wanted to maintain the balance, as they had always done, Kansas would have to be a slave state. However, Kansas was north of the Missouri Compromise line, so legally, it could not be a slave state.

The Kansas-Nebraska Act was a compromise between the two sides. The act set forth that the two new states would be allowed to choose for themselves, a concept called "popular sovereignty", whether they would enter the union as free or slave states. The pro-slavery groups saw this as a big victory as they had the chance to get a state located above the line established by the Missouri Compromise. The free-state forces felt this was an incredible defeat and politically turned on many of the congressmen who voted for the act. While at the time of the passage of the act, it was considered a compromise between the two sides, Congress did not foresee the disaster that this law would inflict on the Kansas and Missouri border. In fact, a lawyer from Illinois named Abraham Lincoln warned that "the contest will come to blows and bloodshed" (Banks 463). Lincoln would be proven correct as the next several years would be times of violent confrontations between pro-slavery and free-stater supporters, guerrilla warfare, murder, robbery, hooliganism, massacres, and the destruction of most of the material wealth in those border counties.

Bleeding Kansas

Most historians consider the Bleeding Kansas Era to have lasted from 1854, with the passage of the Kansas-Nebraska Act, to 1861 with admission to the Union of Kansas as a Free-State and the first shots of the Civil War at Fort Sumter. In reality, the struggle between the residents on the border of Missouri and Kansas would continue until the end of the Civil War in 1865.

The passage of the Kansas-Nebraska Act, in May of 1854, effectively opened Kansas and Nebraska to white settlement. Prior to this event, these territories were largely populated by Native American tribes. With the edict from the government that these two territories, would be allowed to vote as to their free or slave state status before becoming states, the race was on to make sure that each side could get enough "voters" into the state to sway the election. The first election in Kansas would be held in March of 1855. The two factions had roughly ten months to get their supporters in place so they could vote in that election.

Both sides mobilized quickly. In the north, the New England Emigrant Aid Society was chartered in April 1854 in anticipation of the passage of the Kansas-Nebraska Act. The purpose of this group was to help fund free-state settlers from the northeast to make the journey west and settle in Kansas. As mentioned previously, this group and their east coast money are credited with sending hundreds of anti-slavery settlers to the new territory. Locally, many settlers came from Missouri, Iowa, Ohio and Kentucky to settle and create new towns in the Kansas Territory. Towns were usually settled by one faction or the other. Lawrence was settled just months after the passage of the Kansas-Nebraska Act by the New England Aid Society and was known to be an abolitionist stronghold. Leavenworth and Atchison were settled by pro-slavery Missourians and the ideologies of the residents of those communities followed those of their pro-slavery town founders.

For smaller communities, the settlers often set up groups to attempt to maintain law and order, in addition to ensuring that anyone living in their communities was on the "right" side of the slavery question. The Salt Creek Squatters Association was organized for the Salt Creek Valley, a community located just west of Leavenworth. The Salt Creek group established a "vigilance" committee that would ensure that the rules of the association were followed. In Salt Creek, this group also made sure that no "abolitionists" would be allowed to join their community. Think of these groups as "homeowners associations" that also controlled your political beliefs. The Salt Creek Squatters Bylaws lay out their beliefs on slavery and the expectation that if you wanted to settle in their community, you were expected to share and work to uphold these same views. Below is an excerpt from those bylaws created and approved on June 10, 1854.

(8)   That we recognize the institution of slavery as always existing in this Territory and recommend slaveholders to introduce their property as early as possible.
(9)   That we will afford protection to no Abolitionists as settlers of Kansas Territory
(10)   that a "Vigilance committee" of thirteen be appointed by the Chairman to decide upon all disputes in relation to claims, and to protect the rightful party; and for that purpose, shall have power to call together the entire "Squatter's Association."
(11)   That all persons who wish to become members of the Squatter's Association shall subscribe to the foregoing preamble and resolutions (Hall 214)

Due to the lack of organization in Kansas following the opening of the territory, most of the problems in Kansas can largely be attributed to bands of "pro-slavery" men, sometimes called Bushwhackers or Border Ruffians. These groups were comprised mostly of Missourians coming into Kansas intending to influence elections or to intimidate Kansas settlers to either leave the state or to vote for pro-slavery candidates. At the same time, while some of the actual settlers that came to Kansas, came with the goal of influencing the election, most were more concerned with trying to plant crops, start businesses and build homes where their families could live safely and peacefully. In the early days of Kansas, the preponderance of its' residents were preoccupied with trying to survive and were thus not heavily involved in most of the nefarious acts committed in the name of determining the slave status of the state. The free-state supporters of Kansas were not completely innocent, but most of the actions taken during this period were committed by pro-slavery forces.

The first significant milestone in the settling of Kansas was the first election, which was held in November 1854. The purpose of this election was to elect a "non-voting" delegate to the U.S. Congress from the Kansas Territory. This election was a bit of a disaster and fraught with fraud. Many pro-slavery supporters crossed over the border to vote in the Kansas election even though they had no legal standing in the state. These "Border Ruffians" would influence this election greatly and succeed in electing a pro-slavery candidate, John Wilkins Whitfield, to that post. A congressional investigation the next year determined that over 60% of the votes cast in that election were "fraudulent". In one location, only 20 of the 604 votes cast were by actual citizens of Kansas (Cutler).

The next election was held four months later in March of 1855. This election, which would choose state delegates to the Kansas Territorial Government, played out very similarly to the previous one. More than 6,000 votes were cast in this election for a territory that, at the time, claimed only around 3,000 residents. Not surprisingly, 37 of the 39 territorial seats went to pro-slavery candidates. Territorial Governor Andrew Reeder, who came to Kansas with pro-slavery beliefs, was responsible for validating the results of the election. After considering the action of the border ruffians, Governor Andrew Reeder would switch sides and become a free-sate proponent.

Figure 6: Territorial Governor Andrew Reeder, Image courtesy of Kansas State Historical Society

Not only would he switch allegiances, but he also invalidated the results from the election in five districts, calling for a re-vote in those districts on May 22nd. With stricter controls around the May 22nd election, eight of the eleven men elected from these five districts were free-staters. Pro-slavery representatives still held a 29 – 10 voting advantage (Olsen).

Governor Reeder was concerned that having the territorial capital too close to the Missouri border would allow Missourians to have too much influence on the action of the governing body. He decided to name Pawnee, Kansas, a small town near Fort Riley as the new Territorial Capital. Governor Reeder just happened to have done a bit of land speculation in the Pawnee area. It was in Pawnee, in July 1855,

Figure 7: Left: Now a ghost-town, Pawnee, KS served as the Territorial Capital for 5 days in July 1855. Right: First Territorial Capitol, Pawnee, KS. Image courtesy of Kansas State Historical Society

that the newly elected delegates held their first meeting. The first order of business for this decidedly pro-slavery body was to invalidate the results from the May 22nd election and re-seat the delegates that were displaced due to that election. The next order of business was to move the capital to the Shawnee Methodist Indian Mission, which was located two miles from the Missouri border near what is today Fairway, Kansas. Reconvening a week later at the Shawnee Indian Mission the delegates started passing pro-slavery laws that would closely follow those in place in Missouri. The laws passed by the new legislative body included the death penalty for helping a slave run away. Voting and jury service depended on a person's willingness to return an escaped slave. Making statements that questioned someone's right to own slaves was punishable by up to two years in prison. The Shawnee Indian Mission would be the capital for less than a month, holding that title from July 16 through August 7, 1855. It was then moved to Lecompton, Kansas, a strong pro-slavery settlement just miles from the abolitionist city of Lawrence. It was chosen as the new capital likely as a compromise with free-state members as it moved the capital to be farther away from Missouri influences, but also placed it in a decidedly pro-slavery community.

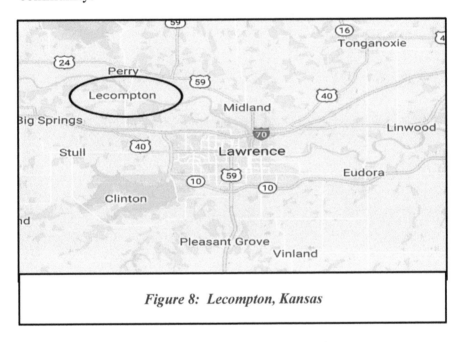

Figure 8: Lecompton, Kansas

Understandably, free-state leaders were not pleased with the first two elections and the resulting laws that were passed by the pro-slavery delegates, now based in Lecompton. The free-staters in Kansas called the current elected officials' meeting in Lecompton the "Bogus Legislature". In August of 1855, they gathered in Topeka to form their own government which would stand in opposition to the pro-slavery government led by this Bogus Legislature. In December of 1855, these free-staters approved their own territorial constitution, called the Topeka Constitution. This constitution was submitted to the U.S. Senate, but rejected because the legislative body in Topeka was not recognized by the U.S. Government.

The violence of the Bleeding Kansas era was turned up a notch in November of 1855, by an event commonly referred to as the Wakarusa War. The term "war" in the name is misleading, as there were no large battles or even skirmishes in this "war". The Wakarusa River is a small stream located south of Lawrence, flowing east, where it eventually meets the Kansas River, in Douglas County, at Eudora. In a small settlement that no longer exists called Hickory Point, Franklin Coleman shot and killed Charles Dow over a property line dispute. The Hickory Point settlement at this time was made up of about 100 free-state families and about 15 pro-slavery families. Coleman, the killer, was a pro-slavery man, and Dow, the deceased, was a free-stater (Litteer 7). Immediately after the killing of Dow, his friend Jacob Branson started gathering other free-state men and rallied them to go and get Coleman and make him pay for his actions.

Unbeknownst to this group, Coleman, fearing for his safety, had gone almost immediately and turned himself in to the Douglas County Sheriff, Samuel J. Jones. Jones, a pro-slavery Missouri resident who had arrived on the border in 1854, had been appointed Douglas County Sheriff in 1855. He would use his office to aggressively enforce the pro-slavery laws passed by the Bogus Legislature. Sheriff Jones, upon advice from new Territorial Governor Wilson Shannon, held Coleman in Lecompton for several days waiting on the arrival of a judge, who would release him on $500 bail.

Meanwhile, back in Hickory Point, Branson and

Figure 9: Sheriff Samuel Jones

about 30 other vigilantes had ransacked Coleman's house while searching for Coleman only to learn of his surrender to Sheriff Jones. This infuriated the free-state men and a few days later on the 26th of November these men met in front of Coleman's house, where they circled around the bloody spot in the road where Dow was murdered. Speeches were made, and the group was whipped into a frenzy. The result of this event was that Coleman's and a Mr. Buckley's cabin were burned to the ground. Buckley was a friend of Coleman's who had accompanied him when he turned himself into Sheriff Jones.

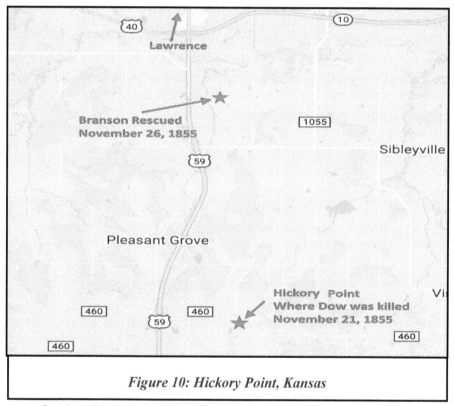

Figure 10: Hickory Point, Kansas

After hearing about this incident, Sheriff Jones found a pro-slavery justice of the peace who signed a warrant for the arrest of Jacob Branson for threatening the life of Buckley. Jones and his posse of about 16 men went to Hickory Point to arrest Branson, which they did. On the way back to Lawrence, Jones and his men were stopped on the Hickory Point road by a large group of Free-Staters who feared for Branson's safety since he was a witness against Coleman. The free-staters demanded that Branson be released. Jones refused, contending that he had a warrant for his arrest. After about a 30-minute standoff, Jones, seeing that he did not have the numbers to resist, turned Branson over to the free-staters. Before turning and riding away, Sheriff Jones yelled at Branson that he would "be sorry" and that he would be back after he asked the Governor for reinforcements. Governor Shannon agreed to Jones' request and called out the militia to report to Sheriff Jones. The militia at this time was largely composed of Missouri Ruffians (Blackmar 855).

Knowing that Jones would be gathering men in Missouri, the town of Lawrence set about preparing for an invasion. The townsfolks put up barricades at the entry points to the town and started military drills for all men who were willing to fight. Jones did indeed gather a small army and would take this army of 1500 men, comprised mostly of Missourians, both militiamen and civilians, to the outskirts of Lawrence where Branson was staying for protection against the Sheriff.

Jones and his men were camped just south of town on the Wakarusa River. This weeklong siege of the city, which was ended by a truce brokered by Governor Shannon, would become known as the Wakarusa War. There was only one casualty during the Wakarusa War. Thomas Barber, an abolitionist, was shot on his way to help defend Lawrence. Barber's death is memorialized in a poem by John Greenleaf Whittier titled *"Burial of Barber"*. Whittier's poem would be published widely in east coast newspapers bringing "Bleeding Kansas" to the rest of the country.

Lawrence had not seen the last of the Border Ruffians.

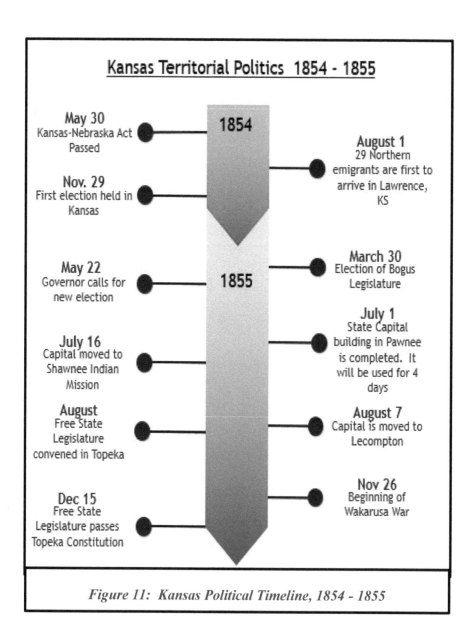

Figure 11: Kansas Political Timeline, 1854 - 1855

In January of 1856, the free-state men in Kansas held their own, non-sanctioned election. Not surprisingly, a full slate of free-state officials was elected, including Charles Robinson as Governor. This meant that the Kansas Territory now had two functioning governments, with very different views of how to govern. This presented a dilemma for residents of the new territory. There were two governments each with their own version of laws which in many cases directly contradicted each other. Which laws should they follow?

Even though the Topeka Legislature had significant backing in the northern states and despite a federal panel of experts who had determined that the pro-slavery legislature was illegally formed due to rampant voter fraud, U.S. President Franklin Pierce refused to recognize

Figure 12: Charles Robinson, elected Free-State Governor in January 1856. Image courtesy of Kansas Historical Society

the Free-State Legislature and, in fact, went as far as to say that these men were insurrectionists. President Pierce favored pro-slavery views, even though he was from New Hampshire.

In May of 1856, Sheriff Jones would be shot in Lawrence while serving warrants on men who were deemed to have participated in the Free-State Legislature, a body that the Federal Government had determined was interfering with the work of the actual Kansas Territorial Legislature in Lecompton. Sheriff Jones survived the assassination attempt and would exact his revenge, when on May 21st he and David Atchison, U.S. Senator from Missouri and namesake of the town of Atchison Kansas, would show up on the outskirts of Lawrence with around 800 pro-slavery men from both Kansas and

Missouri. Atchison, a skilled orator would encourage his men to "never to slacken or stop until every spark of free-state, free-speech, free-n*****, or free in any shape is quenched out of Kansaz! [sic] (E. Anderson)."

These men would leave Lawrence, whose residents did not resist, in shambles. Printing presses were destroyed, and the Free-State Hotel was burned to the ground. While the town was thoroughly ransacked and a significant amount of property was stolen, no Lawrence residents were injured. The *Lecompton Union* newspaper reported this event with this headline: "Lawrence Taken! – Glorious Triumph of the Law-and-Order over Fanaticism in Kansas!" Kansas was deeply divided at this point in history.

Figure 13: David Rice Atchison, U.S. Senator and pro-slavery supporter

Figure 14: Drawing of Lawrence after the first raid. Image courtesy of the Kansas State Historical Society

The Violence Escalates

New Kansas resident, John Brown, who would achieve infamy in American history books for his raid on Harper's Ferry in Virginia, retaliated for the sacking of Lawrence with a massacre at Pottawatomie Creek. He and his men would literally hack five pro-slavery settlers to pieces with swords.

John Brown had come to Kansas in October 1855, from the northeast to be with his sons who were living in Osawatomie. Brown had created his own army by fathering 20 children, all of whom shared his radical abolitionist views. Brown, even though he is known for supporting the worthy cause of the abolition of slavery, was responsible for some of the worst acts ever committed during the Bleeding Kansas era. Brown is the focal point of the mural, *Tragic Prelude*, painted by John Steuart Curry, located in the Kansas Statehouse in Topeka. Brown would only spend three years in Kansas, but definitely left his mark in that short time.

The settlers that Brown and his men murdered near Pottawatomie Creek, near Lane, Kansas, were not slave owners and had nothing to do with the sacking of Lawrence. Their "crime" was being known as pro-slavery men. John Doyle, son and brother of three of the men killed in Brown's raid, described the attack this way;

Figure 15: Tragic Prelude, by John Steuart Curry. Image courtesy of Kansas State Historical Society

Figure 16: The Pottawatomie Massacre occurred near Lane, Kansas, on the night of May 24, 1856.

I found my father and one brother (William) lying dead in the road, about two hundred yards from the house. I saw my other brother lying dead on the ground, about one hundred and fifty yards from the house, in the grass near a ravine. His fingers were cut off; his head was cut open; there was a hole in his breast. William's head was cut open, and a hole was in his jaw, as though it was made by a knife, and a hole was also in his side. My father was shot in the forehead and stabbed in the breast. (U.S. Congress 108)

The ferocity with which John Brown and his men had executed these men shocked the nation. After the massacre at Pottawatomie Creek, Brown would claim that he was "an agent of the Lord, assigned to punish those who favored slavery" (Blum 309).

In a letter to family, Kansas settler Edward Bridgeman describes the situation in Kansas in the spring of 1856 this way;

In some small towns, the men are called up nearly every night to hold themselves in readiness to meet the worst as scouting parties of Alabamians, Georgians and Missourians that are around continually, plundering clothes yards, horses and cattle, and everything they can lay hold of. A few miles from Lawrence a man was plowing, and a party of Southerners came along and being hungry killed his best ox, ate what they wanted, took away some and left the rest. Such like occurrences are almost daily taking place.

Tuesday, 27. Since I wrote the above, the Osawatomie company has returned to O [sic]. As news came that we could do nothing immediately, so we returned back. On our way back we heard that 5 men had been killed by Free-State men. The men were butchered -- ears cut off and the bodies thrown into the river. The murdered men (pro-slavery) had thrown out threats and insults, yet the act was barbarous and inhuman whoever committed by. (Bridgman, 1856)

Brown's massacre at Pottawatomie Creek opened the flood gates for both sides to begin widespread guerrilla operations.   The Kansas guerilla bands were known as Jayhawkers and the Missouri groups were referred to first as "Border Ruffians" and then later as Bushwhackers. Many of the Kansas bands were organized as Kansas Militia units tasked with "protecting" the free-state settlers from pro-slavery forces. These Kansas Militia units would also raid pro-slavery settlements and bring back supplies. Supplies for free-state communities were difficult to come by because the Border Ruffians were robbing and destroying any shipments meant for free-state communities.   Many free-state settlements were on the verge of starvation and the only way to procure these necessary supplies was to raid pro-slavery towns where supplies were still flowing freely. While there were legitimate actions taken by the Kansas Militia, many of these units quickly devolved into simple guerrilla bands as the temptation to rob and plunder the homes of their enemies became too great a temptation for the men to resist.

The leaders of these groups were reviled as devils on one side of the argument and looked upon as heroes on the other. Remember that at this point, in 1856, it was not strictly a Missouri verse Kansas issue. There were both free-state and pro-slavery communities scattered across the Kansas eastern border.   A Missouri newspaper described James Lane, a notorious Jayhawker, this way, ".... an evil looking creature with the sad, dim-eyed, bad toothed face of a harlot. A cynical, unscrupulous demagogue, Lane used, without the least hesitation any and every kind of chicanery and skullduggery to gain his political and personal ends" (Brophy 15). On the other hand, a free-state newspaper, the *Daily Argus* from Rock Island, Illinois, announced a Lane speech this way; "General J. H. Lane of Kansas, the chivalrous defender of the liberties of that down-trodden territory will speak in the courthouse yard to-night" (2).

The Free-State Legislature was scheduled to meet again at Constitution Hall in Topeka in July of 1856. President Pierce informed the leaders that this was an illegal gathering and that steps would be taken to disband the group if they proceeded to meet. To that end, Colonel Edwin Sumner, who was known as a soldier who would follow orders without question, was sent to Fort Riley with four companies of soldiers who would be ready if the free-state men convened the meeting.

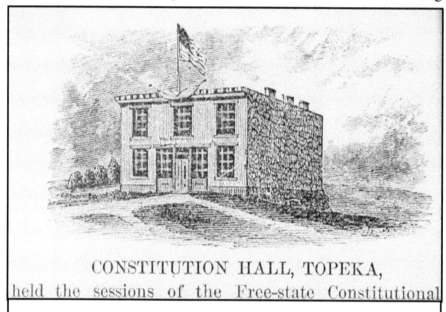

CONSTITUTION HALL, TOPEKA,

held the sessions of the Free-state Constitutional

Figure 17: Constitution Hall, Topeka, Kansas. Image Courtesy of the Kansas State Historical Society

At eight o'clock on the morning of July 4, 1856, the Free-State Legislature called to order their legislative session. Shortly thereafter, Colonel Sumner and his soldiers quickly made their way to Constitution Hall, where he walked into both the House and Senate chambers and delivered this speech:

Gentlemen, I am called upon this day to perform the most painful duty of my life. Under the authority of the President's proclamation, I am here to disperse the legislature, and I therefore inform you that you cannot meet. I, therefore, in accordance with my orders, command you to disperse.

Asked by one of the attendees if the legislature was being dispersed at the point of a bayonet? Sumner would reply, "I shall use all the forces under my command to carry out my orders." The Legislature then abandoned their meeting and dispersed as requested (Bisel 77).

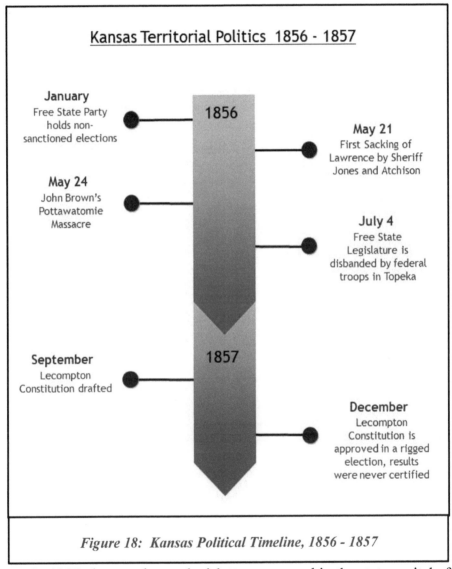

Kansas Territorial Politics 1856 - 1857

January
Free State Party holds non-sanctioned elections

1856

May 21
First Sacking of Lawrence by Sheriff Jones and Atchison

May 24
John Brown's Pottawatomie Massacre

July 4
Free State Legislature is disbanded by federal troops in Topeka

September
Lecompton Constitution drafted

1857

December
Lecompton Constitution is approved in a rigged election, results were never certified

Figure 18: Kansas Political Timeline, 1856 - 1857

In 1857, the pro-slavery legislature convened in the state capital of Lecompton. At this convention, the delegates drafted a pro-slavery constitution called the Lecompton Constitution. The Lecompton Constitution was written in response to the anti-slavery, Topeka

Constitution, that had been created by free-state men in their first convention in 1855. The Topeka Constitution was created by an unsanctioned body and was never accepted as the law of the land. The Lecompton Constitution, while it had the support of the existing Kansas Government, was never officially approved by the voters of Kansas. It was approved by a rigged election in December of 1857, but the results of this election were never approved due to the known fraud in the process.

On January 4, 1858, Kansas voters rejected the Lecompton Constitution by a count of 10,226 to 138. It would be voted down again later that same year in August, which would signal the beginning of the end for pro-slavery control of the state government. In 1858, the newly appointed Territorial Governor, John W. Geary, with the help of federal troops, managed to gain some control over the border region. By 1859,

Figure 19: Constitution Hall, Lecompton, Kansas. Site of the Lecompton Constitutional Convention in 1857

the government was now in the control of the free-state supporters. This would lead to the approval of the Wyandotte Constitution, created by Free-State Legislators, which abolished slavery and eventually led to Kansas becoming the 34th state in 1861.

During the Bleeding Kansas era, the Kansas/Missouri border residents were in a constant state of fear. The early battles in 1855 and 1856 led to the development of the guerrilla bands on both sides of the slavery issue.   The timelines shown in this chapter only show key events. In reality, the border counties were constantly being raided by a multitude of guerrilla bands from both sides of the state line. That said, property crimes and politically driven misdeeds were the major issues facing Kansas residents during this time frame. The Federal Government, likely trying to justify later actions, published a study in 1859 which reported that over 200 men died during 1855-1856. Later studies have shown this number to be greatly exaggerated with the actual number being closer to 42 (Erwin 20).

At various times both sides also dealt with occupying forces from the federal government. Remember that from 1855 to mid-1858, the recognized Kansas Government was pro-slavery and the Federal Government supported the laws enacted by that government. That ended in 1859 when the free-state delegates were able to take control of the legislature. After control of the legislature changed sides, the Federal Army, in effect, switched sides because the official government position on slavery did the same. The fact that the free-staters were taking control of the government, did not, however, lessen the frequency of raids on both sides of the state line.

As the free-state group was becoming stronger the number of raids into Missouri to "free slaves" would increase. In February of 1859, Kansas Territorial Governor, Samuel Mediary issued the Amnesty Act which was described as "an act to establish peace in Kansas". This act basically wiped out all charges for any abolitionist's acts perpetrated in Kansas during the Bleeding Kansas era. For men like Jim Lane, James Montgomery and Charles "Doc" Jennison, this only made them bolder and it became more and more common for bands of Kansans to go into Missouri with the sole purpose of finding slaves and bringing them back to Kansas where they could be free (Rafiner 107). Of course, if wholesale stealing and burning happened at the same time, so be it.

Pro-slavery men on both sides of the state line opposed these raids and since slavery was still legal in Missouri, these acts were also a violation of current Missouri law. So again, we had one group trying to free slaves and the other group doing their best to stop that group by arresting these men and turning them in to the authorities in Missouri for theft of property.

One incident that will give readers an idea of the atmosphere of Kansas in 1859 occurred in January. John Doy was leading a group of men who had "freed" thirteen slaves from Missouri and was leading them to Lawrence when the whole group was arrested by a pro-slavery posse from Kansas. The posse took the men to Weston, Missouri, where Doy was tried and sentenced to five years in prison. Before being moved to a Missouri prison, a group of free-state men from Lawrence rode into Weston, broke Doy out of jail, and escorted him back to Lawrence (Bisel 97). The lawlessness on display in this story is just "another day in Kansas" during this period.

Allen T. Ward, a Paola, Kansas resident, in a letter to his sister had this to say about the situation in Kansas:

> . . . *the worst feature in this war is the predatory or guerrilla bands that infest the country—For instance, a jayhawker (or robber) here in Kansas will get up a party and dash over into Missouri, and wherever they can find any property worth bringing away they appropriate it to themselves. Negro's, horses, cattle, sheep and hogs are all driven off, stores robbed and even the clothing of women and children have been frequently taken; this calls for revenge and retaliation of the other party: then in turn a party of Missourians will make a raid on some unprotected place in Kansas, plunder the stores, and take off whatever they can that is valuable. And so it goes, the parties are no ways particular who they rob. The object is plunder—I know men here who have become wealthy just by the horses and cattle they have stolen. If a man has an enemy, all he has to do to get rid of him is to say to a jayhawker that he is a secessionist, or he sympathizes with the South, and the man is robbed of all he has and either driven off or hung. (1861)*

A Kansas private likely riding with Jim Lane's outfit, said it this way, "The tables are turned now; and here in camp are many Kansas men who were hunted in '55 and '56 by the Border Ruffians who rode, booted, and spurred over our state." These men intended "settle old scores" (Rafiner 117).

On the Missouri side, particularly with the beginning of the Civil War in 1861, the Federal Army acted as an occupying force in the Missouri border counties. Many residents of Missouri changed sides during the war due to the actions of the Federal Army and its soldiers who, oftentimes, acted worse than the guerrillas. The state of life in Missouri at this time will be discussed in the next chapter.

This entire era was one in which each side was constantly doing something to avenge some terrible act perpetrated by the other side. At some point throughout the Bleeding Kansas era, this became so commonplace that both sides likely forgot what they were avenging, and it just became a way of life. There are many stories from both sides of the border of guerrilla bands who didn't particularly care what side a person was on; they were just out to destroy and steal property. The taking of human lives was just part of the game. Arguably, by the time the Civil War began in 1861 the fight on the Kansas and Missouri border was not about slavery or state's rights, rather, it was about revenge.

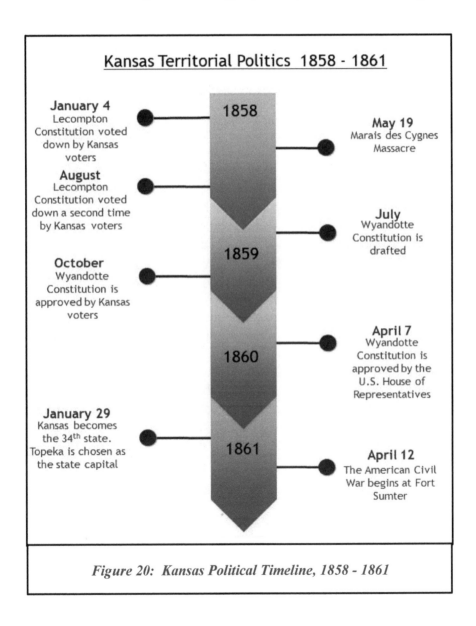

Figure 20: Kansas Political Timeline, 1858 - 1861

Kansas Constitution Comparison

	Topeka (Free-State)	Lecompton (Pro-Slavery)	Leavenworth (Free-State)	Wyandotte (Free-State)
Allowed Slavery	No	Yes	No	No
Votes for Women	No	No	No	Only for School Boards
Votes for Blacks	No	No	Yes	No

Figure 21: Comparison of Kansas Constitutions

The chart on the following page shows a sampling of the engagements that occurred between the two sides during the 1855 – 1861 period. This is not a complete list and several smaller events are not included. However, the list does show the way the aggressor in the Border War changed over time. The Jayhawkers becoming the primary aggressors in late 1858 is what gave power and acceptance to groups like Quantrill's on the Missouri side. By 1860, the Jayhawkers were often acting as part of the U.S. Army, which meant that their actions were larger and more organized. The actions by Missourian's paled in scale to those attributed to the Jayhawkers as they were perpetrated by smaller independent bands, rather than large organized forces. The actions of Jayhawkers like Lane, Montgomery and Jennison solidified Missouri's hatred of "anything Kansas" by the end of the war. Before this time, the line was drawn at pro-slavery versus free-state with men on each side living in both Kansas and Missouri. By the end of the war, the divide had shifted to Missouri versus Kansas.

Date	Event	Leader	Aggressor
December '55	Wakarusa War, KS	Sherriff Jones	Pro-Slavery
May 21, '56	Atchison raids Lawrence, KS	David Atchison	Pro-Slavery
May 24, '56	Pottawatomie Massacre, KS	John Brown	Abolitionists
June 2, '56	Battle of Blackjack, KS	Pate vs Brown	Both Sides
August 30, '56	Battle of Osawatomie, KS	Colonel Reid	Pro-Slavery
February 11, '58	Raid of Fort Scott, KS	Montgomery	Jayhawkers
May 19, '58	Marais des Cygnes Massacre, KS	Hamilton	Pro-Slavery
December 20,'58	Raid of Vernon County, MO	John Brown	Abolitionist
November '60	Bates County, MO	Jennison	Jayhawkers
June 19, 1861	Independence	Jennison	Jayhawkers
July 20, 1861	Morristown, MO	Jennison	Jayhawkers
July 26, 1861	Harrisonville, MO	Jennison	Jayhawkers
Sept 17, 1861	Morristown, MO	Montgomery	Jayhawkers
Sept 19, 1861	Papinville, MO	Lane	Jayhawkers
Sept 26, 1861	Osceola, MO	Lane	Jayhawkers
Oct 14, 1861	Humboldt, KS	Livingston	CSA
Oct 16, 1861	Pleasant Hill, MO	Lane	Jayhawkers
Oct 17, 1861	Kingsville, MO	Lane	Jayhawkers
Oct 18, 1861	Rose Hill, MO	Lane	Jayhawkers
Oct 20, 1861	Clinton, MO	Lane	Jayhawkers
Oct 21, 1861	Humansville, MO	Lane	Jayhawkers
Oct 1861	Pleasant Hill, MO	Lane	Jayhawkers
Oct 22, 1861	Gardner, KS	Yeager	Bushwhackers
Nov 14, 1861	Independence, MO	Jennison/Anthony	Jayhawkers
Nov 22, 1861	Pleasant Hill, MO	Jennison/Anthony	Jayhawkers
Nov 1861	West Point, MO	Jennison/Anthony	Jayhawkers
Dec 1861	Morristown, MO	Jennison Anthony	Jayhawkers
Dec 11, 1861	Potosi, KS	Clement	Bushwhackers
Dec 12, 1861	Papinville, MO	Stewart	Jayhawkers
Dec 12, 1861	Butler, MO	Stewart	Jayhawkers

Figure 22:   Brief list of Border Raids prior to the raid on Olathe. Events highlighted in butternut are those where pro-slavery/Bushwhackers were the aggressors. Events in blue are those where the free-staters/Jayhawkers were the aggressors.

Life in the western Missouri border counties in the early 1850s was pretty good. The population, and thus the economy, were growing rapidly, largely due to western expansion and the location of the border counties at the eastern end of the wagon trails going west. The California, Sante Fe and Oregon Trails all began in the Kansas City area at this time. The trail traffic both from the east and back from the west meant that all sorts of business was conducted at the terminus of those trails in the western Missouri counties. Many travelers were headed west, and those travelers needed food, tools, clothing, wagons, horses, farming implements, etc. The shop keepers of the border counties were more than happy to sell these travelers the goods they needed for their journey. In 1850 the population of the three most populous Missouri border counties, Jackson, Cass and Bates, was estimated at 20,120

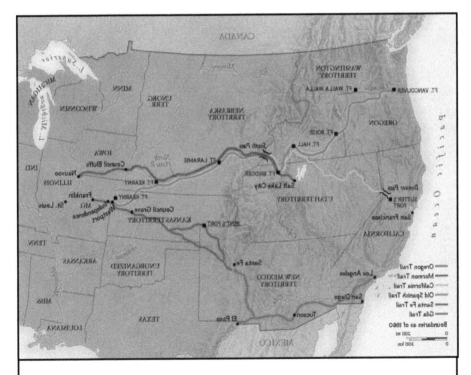

Figure 23: 1860 Trails West, Image courtesy of National Geographic

whites. It is estimated that at this time there were as many as 3,000 slaves in Jackson County, 500 in Cass County and 150 in Bates County. By 1854 the white population would grow to 24,520 with Jackson

County being the largest, accounting for 55% of that population. Bates County was the least populated of the three accounting for 18% of the population. At this point, 87% of the area's population was either Missourians or people from other southern states, mainly Kentucky, Virginia and Tennessee (Rafiner 67).

While there are no numbers to prove this, it is likely that many of the pro-slavery men who ventured into Kansas to fraudulently vote for Kansas to be a slave state would have been from this border region. There would have been others who journeyed from farther east in Missouri and still others who hailed from many other southern states, but the majority would likely have come from the border area. Remember that in these early days of the Kansas Territory, many of the early settlers in Kansas had Missouri roots. There was no bad blood at this point between Missouri and Kansas, rather, the conflict was about whether Kansas would be a "slave state", or a "free-state".

There were many people on both sides of the question from both Missouri and Kansas. The more densely populated areas like Jackson County would have seen a fairly even split between the two factions, while the more rural areas would have been predominantly pro-slavery. There would have been people on both sides in most of the border counties. At this time, in Missouri, people from both sides of the issue would have lived side by side, gone to church together, helped each other build barns and harvest crops. The animosity started with the Kansas-Nebraska Act in 1854, was nurtured during the Bleeding Kansas era, and then intensified by the events that occurred after the beginning of the Civil War.

Tensions began to rise in 1856 with the first sacking of Lawrence and then John Brown's retaliatory Pottawatomie massacre. Brown's actions rallied the pro-slavery forces and the murders perpetrated during that event raised the stakes in the free verse slave debate. Missouri Border Ruffians would respond to the Pottawatomie Massacre in August of 1856 by attacking Osawatomie, Kansas. Border Ruffian John Reid and his 250 to 400 men would briefly battle John Brown before Brown's retreat. Once Brown had withdrawn his troops, the town was almost completely destroyed with any items of value being taken by the pro-slavery group.

This back and forth would continue for the next two years with the venom between the two sides growing with each and every attack by the other. The political tide began to turn in early 1859 as the free-state men in Kansas were beginning to take control of the government and thus the military in the state. With the ideological shift in the state, many of the anti-slavery leaders, such as Jennison and Montgomery, began to focus on making sure that all pro-slavery men were forcibly expelled from the state.

   This tactic by the Jayhawkers meant that there were masses of Kansas pro-slavery refugees fleeing Kansas for a safer location in the western Missouri counties. Some of these refugees would continue

Figure 24: Map of the Missouri/Kansas Border, 1860

through the border counties and move further east to get further away from the turmoil of the area, but many would stay in the westernmost counties of Missouri. A Butler, Missouri, resident said, "It is impossible to give you an idea of the affairs as they exist. Their numbers [Kansas refugees] are increasing every hour". A Cass County resident reported:

Every vacant house and shed is filled with these unfortunate people – three and four families in a single hut – who are in a destitute condition, and for food to sustain life solely rely upon the charity of Missourians" (Goodrich 215).

This influx of refugees meant that these Missouri border counties were now even more heavily populated with pro-slavery supporters. Not only were these exiles pro-slavery supporters, but they were angry and had a score to settle.

In efforts to settle that score, many of them would form bands of armed men who would go back across the state line into Kansas to exact revenge. After getting their revenge, they would retreat to Missouri often being chased by armed Kansans. This made it appear that Missourians were the crux of the problem, even though many of the groups crossing the border were comprised of "ex-Kansans" (Rafiner 102). This is also the point in history when the Missouri "Border Ruffians" began to be commonly called "Bushwhackers".

After the beginning of the Civil War in 1861, the western border and much of the state of Missouri was a mess. Officially, Missouri was a Union state, even though most of the government, including the Governor and a large percentage of the population, strongly supported the southern cause. In the 1860 Presidential election, Abraham Lincoln received only 10% of the Missouri vote. In some counties, such as Vernon, Lincoln received zero votes. In fact, Missouri was represented with a star on the official Confederate flag, "Stars and Bars" even though the state never officially seceded from the Union. The star was added in recognition of the unofficial government set up by Governor Sterling Price a few months into the war. As one can imagine this caused some problems for the people trying to live in the state. Shortly after the onset of war, in the fall of 1861, men like Lane, Jennison and Montgomery would take advantage of the chaos in Missouri by continually raiding and destroying Missouri towns and farms. (See the chart of events in the previous chapter)

We will spend more time on Lane and Jennison in future chapters, but these two men and their armies, under the guise of being Union Army troops, would spend most of the latter part of 1861 in western Missouri leaving a trail of carnage wherever they went. Murder, robbery, looting and destruction were the tools that they used in their effort to make Missourians pay for supporting the Confederacy. It did not matter that Missouri was officially a Union state. During this brief period, the Jayhawkers would destroy over 15 Missouri communities, some of which would never recover and now no longer exist. Jim Lane's troops alone are estimated to have looted and plundered between

Figure 25: Official Flag of the Confederate States of American in November 1861. The stars on the flag include stars for Missouri and Kentucky even though those states did not officially secede. The flag known today with the diagonal blue stripes and stars was never the official flag of the Confederate Government. The better-known flag was only used as a battle flag and was never recognized as the official flag of the Confederacy

1600 and 2400 farms in the fall of 1861 (Rafiner 142).

The situation in western Missouri in the first years of the war was that many, but not all, Unionists, mainly from Kansas City, Westport and Independence had already fled to the east due to danger from the Bushwhackers and attacks by their southern sympathizing neighbors. Southern Sympathizers were constantly on the lookout for Jayhawkers and the federal forces, who oftentimes were one and the same. One resident described Westport this way:

Westport was once a thriving town, with large storage, elegant private dwellings and a fine large hotel. Now soldiers are quartered in the dwellings and horses occupy the storerooms. The hotel was burned down three days ago. The houses are torn to pieces,

plastering off, the mantles used to build fires, and doors unhinged.
I presume the place will be burned down as soon as the troops leave.
(Erwin 70)

It was the actions of these Kansas Jayhawkers that focused the animosity of most Missourians, against the state of Kansas regardless of whether they were pro-slavery or anti-slavery. While these Kansans officially rode for the Union, it was hard for many Missouri Union supporters to support the atrocities inflicted on fellow Missourians by these men. Eventually, even the commanders of the Union forces could no longer stomach the actions of these men. Many of the men who led these Jayhawker units would be censured or court-martialed by the Union Army leadership for their actions while on these jayhawking sprees.

The Key Combatants

"History is written by the victors." This quote, generally attributed to Winston Churchill, was more likely first used by Hermann Goring during the Nuremberg trials after the conclusion of World War II. One could easily make an argument that this quote applies to the Border War in Kansas and Missouri. For the most part, the players on the Kansas side tend to be portrayed as patriots trying to save their state from the evils of slavery. On the other hand, the Missouri combatants are commonly seen as criminals, outlaws, backwoods rubes and bloodthirsty devils. In the next few chapters, I have tried to present a balanced view of several of the key figures in the Missouri/Kansas Border War.

The men on each side saw themselves as "soldiers" that fought for their cause. It was important to some that the public and history saw them as soldiers simply following orders, defending their homes and fighting the enemy. Unfortunately, the temptation of taking valuables for personal gain and committing atrocities in the name of their cause took most of them down a darker path. In hindsight, many of the actions by these guerillas, on both sides, seem to be more criminal than having any strategic impact on the war. After the first few months of guerrilla fighting on the border, the raids conducted by each side had more to do with revenge than anything else. The reader must remember that to many of these men, joining one of these raiding bands was the only defense they felt they had to protect their homes and possessions.

Although there is some dispute of this fact, the origins of the word Jayhawk likely comes from a combination of the blue jay; a noisy, quarrelsome bird known to rob nests, and the sparrow hawk; a stealthy hunter. I think it would be fair to say that most Kansans focus on the "stealthy hunter" part of the definition while Missourians focus on the noisy, quarrelsome robber component of the definition. Despite the negative connotation of the origin of the word, Kansans have embraced the Jayhawk, or Jayhawker as a part of the history of their state. The University of Kansas named the Jayhawk as their mascot in 1912.

While Jayhawkers had nothing to do with the raid of Olathe in 1862, it is important to understand what was happening leading up to that night in September 1862.

The Kansas Jayhawkers enjoyed one big advantage over the Missouri Bushwhackers during the years leading up to and during the Civil War. While pro-slavery men had controlled the federal forces and the political machine in Kansas from 1854 – 1858, that changed beginning in late 1858, when anti-slavery forces took control of the state government for good. After this transition of power, the Jayhawkers were often committing their crimes in the name of the federal government, while the Bushwhackers, who were committing very similar acts, were considered outlaws. The leaders of many of the Jayhawk bands were often officers in the Federal Army which added to the "legitimacy" of their actions.

Jayhawkers were an interesting mix of men. Many were volunteers, led by commissioned officers and others were simply opportunists riding with leaders who were also opportunists. There was little difference between the two groups. Peter Bryant, a Lieutenant in the Kansas Militia, described the difference between himself and another man who enlisted in the Federal Army this way:

All the difference between us [the volunteer militia] was he jayhawked under the cover of Uncle Sam and I under a lieutenancy from Governor Robinson. I marched when I damn well pleased; he when he was told to. I kept my plunder (if I chose); he didn't. I took my pay as I went along; he, when he could get it. I have disbanded my squad; he has got to stick here until the war is over. (Goodrich, Black Flag 21)

Another Jayhawker, Webster Moses, described living the high life of a Jayhawker in a letter to his girlfriend back in Illinois:

When we were at Lone Jack. . . about 10 of us went out jayhawking. We went before breakfast and stopped at a rich secesh and told them we wanted some breakfast. While they were getting breakfast, we caught their horses and took the best ones. When we came to breakfast, they did not have enough dishes. The negroes sayed [sic] that they had them hid. We asked the Gentleman where they were, and he told us. We found some silverware among the rest. I got the cupps [sic], two silver ladles and two sets spoons. . . . . Some of the *boys got in some places about $100 worth of silver and some got considerable money. (Black Flag 25)*

The opposite of the Jayhawker was the Bushwhacker. A Bushwhacker was part of a group of pro-slavery and Southern Sympathizers who rode and committed many of the same acts that were being committed by the Jayhawkers, simply in the name of the pro-slavery or Confederate side. Bushwhackers went by many names: border ruffians, guerrillas, partisans and prairie wolves to name a few. In 1862, the Confederate government officially named these men "Partisan Rangers" in an attempt to give the bushwhacker groups some military legitimacy. While these groups were largely made up of Missourians, they were certainly not limited to men from the eastern side of the border. There were plenty of Kansans at the time, with pro-southern views, who wanted to "get in" on the raiding and plundering that was happening on both sides of the border. William Quantrill himself, had spent more time as a Kansas resident than a Missouri one by the time the war began. There were also many men on both sides from other states who had come to the region for the adventure and bounty that could be had by riding with a guerrilla band.

The bushwhacker units were generally made up of young men, some as young as 15 or 16, from prosperous families. Their families more than likely owned a slave or two. During this time, part of a family's wealth would come from the fact that they owned slaves. Slaves were property just like horses or livestock. When the Jayhawkers came through and freed a family's slaves, they, in effect, reduced the wealth that the family had worked hard to build. In their

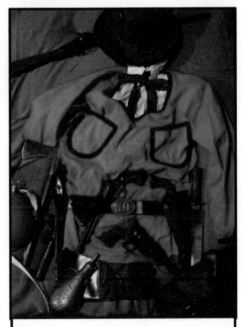

Figure 26: Typical Attire of a Missouri Partisan Ranger. Image courtesy of www.facebook.com/Civil-War-Bushwhackers-and-guerrillas

minds, these young men were fighting to get back what had been stolen from them. To be a Bushwhacker and stay alive, the men had to be expert horsemen and good with a gun. These are skills that would be more prevalent in the upper classes as opposed to poor farmers, who would have had little experience with quality horses and gunplay. In the latter part of 1859, as the anti-slavery faction took power in Kansas, the jayhawking raids into Missouri became more frequent. Due to the destruction exacted on the people and property of Missouri, more young Missourians would join these bushwhacking groups.   Many of these men felt they had no choice but to join a Bushwhacker band to help protect their family and neighbors. They also saw riding with the bushwhackers as a way to recover some of the "property" that they had lost to the Jayhawkers.

One of the most influential and well-known Jayhawkers was James H. Lane, sometimes referred to as "the Liberator of Kansas" or the "Grim Chieftain". Lane's legacy was described by one publication in this way:

Figure 27: James Henry Lane served as a Lieutenant Governor, U.S. House Member and Union General. Image courtesy of the Library of Congress

Only two things were certain; if he [Lane] had ever crossed the border into Missouri and been caught, he would have been hanged from the nearest limb to the tune of merry fiddling and dancing Missourians. The other certainty was when Jim Lane stretched his arms before Kansas and said, "Follow Me" –almost the entire population of Western Kansas would follow him. He was a born leader and a natural fighter. . . . hated in Missouri, loved in Kansas. (Townsend 3)

An Indiana native, Lane, was 41-years-old when he staked a claim to land in Kansas on the outskirts of Lawrence. While living in Indiana, Lane had served as a member of the U.S. House of Representatives and Lieutenant Governor of that state. He was known for his ability to deliver persuasive speeches for large crowds. When he came to Kansas, Lane really did not hold strong beliefs about slavery. His views prior to coming to Kansas are summed up in this quote:

I look upon this nigger question just as I look upon the horse or the jackass questions. It is merely a question of dollars and cents. If Kansas had been a good hemp and tobacco state, I would have favored slavery" (Goodrich, War 50).

He took that sentiment a step further with this quote: "My creed is, let slavery take care of itself. If it can survive the shock of war, let it live" (Bailes 162).

Lane was a person that most people did not really like, but many Kansans were glad he was on their side. To Kansans, he was a necessary evil. Many reports of the time portray Lane as "lacking in moral character". Historian Paul Peterson calls him "an unscrupulous opportunist in both his personal relations and political association. . . violent, paranoid, and highly unbalanced."

The Parkville, Missouri, *Weekly Southern Democrat* said that Lane, "looks only to the present, acts only for today, never gives a thought about how his acts will appear in history." Physically, he

Figure 28: James H. Lane

was a very thin man, referred to as "eely-shaped and extremely homely" by one reporter. He was generally unkept in appearance with his hair flying in all directions. Writer Richard Brownlee describes him as an "evil-looking creature with the sad, dim-eyed, bad toothed face of a harlot" (Soodalter).

After arriving in Kansas, Lane found the abolitionist movement and recognized it as an opportunity to further his wealth and reputation. From this point on, despite his earlier statements to the contrary, Lane became an outspoken free-state man and, in fact, became the face and voice of the movement in the state. In his role as a Kansas abolitionist, and later as a U.S. Senator, Lane often went back east to deliver speeches to raise money for the cause and to convince others to come to Kansas to help in the fight against slavery.

One such speech is summarized by Ronald Soodalter in Missouri Life Magazine:

In 1856, Lane gave a fundraising speech in Chicago on behalf of the free soldiers of Kansas. According to local newspaper accounts, the talk raised an astounding $15,000—more than $400,000 in today's currency—and when he finished, gamblers threw their pistols on the stage and begged Lane to take them west. Businessmen threw their purses, newsboys tossed pennies, women wept, and people milled around the platform in a high state of agitation.

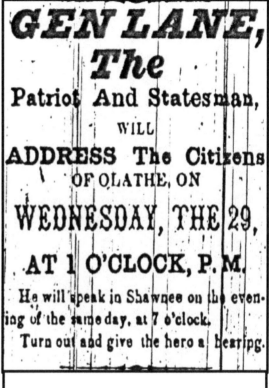

Figure 29: Flyer for Jim Lane speech in Olathe. Published in The Olathe Mirror, October 1862

In 1855, shortly after relocating to Kansas, Lane would serve as the Chairman of the executive committee of the unrecognized, Free-State Legislature that would draft the Topeka Constitution. According to historian Robert Townsend, it was in Topeka that "He [Lane] took command of the entire Free-State movement and planned all-out war against Missouri." It is during this time that Lane is credited with such violent quotes as, "Fight fire with fire, meet the Missourians on their own ground and fight them with their own weapons – an eye for an eye—a tooth for a tooth!", and "Death to the slave hungry Missourians" (Townsend 4).

Lane's personal life was a bit of a mess, his father-in-law, told this story to the *Davenport Democrat*, in the August 27, 1856 edition:

> *. . . [Lane] induced his daughter to go to Kansas he sold her property amounting to $10,000 and after reaching Kansas, Lane procured a mistress and treated his wife so badly that she was forced to leave him for home, and he told her that he had paid her passage on the steamboat to Indiana. When in fact, after the boat started, she found that such was not the case, and it was with a great difficulty that she raised money enough to pay the passage. Lane had robbed her of her whole fortune, been guilty of adultery with a mistress, and sent her home penniless, and after she left tried to get a divorce from her through the very Territorial Legislature, which he is denouncing as bogus and illegal.*

Lane would go back to Indiana a couple of years later and convince his wife to come back to Kansas with him.

A year later, in September of 1856, Lane cemented his name as a skilled military tactician in the minds of free-state Kansans with his

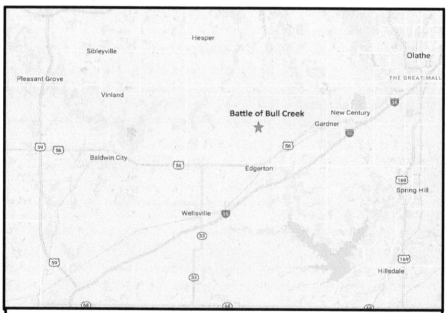

Figure 30: Location of the Battle of Bull Creek in southern Johnson County, Kansas

strategy at the Battle of Bull Creek in southwest Johnson County, Kansas, just north of Edgerton.   Bull Creek was not so much a battle but rather a potential battle that Lane avoided with his clever troop maneuvers.   An estimated proslavery force of 1,600 men had invaded southern Johnson County.   Lane was able to gather up around 200 – 300 men from Topeka and Lawrence and marched them to meet the pro-slavery force.   Knowing that he was vastly outnumbered, Lane positioned his men on a ridge some distance away and then paraded them in such a way that it appeared that they had far more men than were actually present.   Tricked into thinking that they were outnumbered, the leaders of the pro-slavery force packed up and went back to Missouri.

Lane was, without question, was the voice and face of the free-state forces during this time. The stature of Jim Lane in the eyes of the people of Kansas can be seen by the number of things that would bear his name; the towns of Lane and Lanesfield, Lane County, Lane University (now closed), the Lane Trail, and Lane Chimneys were all named in his honor.

In 1861, with the beginning of the Civil War, Lane was appointed Brigadier General by President Lincoln and asked to raise men for the Kansas Volunteers.   This eventually became known as "Lane's Brigade" or the "Kansas Brigade." By July of that year, Lane's Brigade would include the following units:

- 3rd Kansas Volunteer Infantry commanded by Colonel James Montgomery
- 4th Kansas Volunteer Infantry commanded by Colonel William Weer
- 5th Kansas Volunteer Cavalry commanded by Colonel Hampton P. Johnson
- 6th Kansas Volunteer Cavalry commanded by William R Judson
- 7th Kansas Volunteer Cavalry commanded by Colonel Charles R. Jennison
- 8th Kansas Volunteer Infantry commanded by Colonel Henry W. Wessels.

Lane also created the First Kansas Colored Volunteers, which would become the first African American Troops to see combat for the Union army in the Civil War at the Battle of Island Mound in Bates County, Missouri near the town of Butler, MO, in October of 1862.

In 1861, Lane was elected to the U. S. Senate from the new state of Kansas. The fact that he was a Senator and a General at the same time, in addition to the fact that he was a favorite of President Lincoln, gave Lane free reign to use his army as he saw fit on the Missouri/Kansas border. That is exactly what he did.

The first Governor of Kanas, after earning their statehood, was Charles Robinson, the same man who had been elected Governor of the non-official, Free-State Government in 1856. Robinson did not like Lane but had to be careful due to President Lincoln's fondness for the Senator/General. Lincoln was a fan of Lane and felt that Lane was the kind of man who could get things done. Robinson described Lane's activities in this way, "Lane's brigade will get up a war by going over the line, committing depredations, and then returning to our state" (Titterington).

Lane's Brigade was comprised of an interesting group of men, all were volunteers as it was a "volunteer" regiment. Due to this fact, there was little military discipline and order in the command of these men. The reasons that each man had joined the regiment was personal. For some, it may have been to eradicate slavery, but for most, it was probably revenge and the promise of plunder and personal financial reward. An officer of the brigade described the men this way, "a batch of vile vagabonds as unscrupulous and unprincipled as himself [Lane]. Some even still reeking with the filth and odor of the penitentiary" (Fry 71).

Only five months into the Civil War, Lane upped the stakes in the Border War when he took 1,400 of his men into Missouri. His reason for going into Missouri was to punish every community which had given aid to the 12,000 member Missouri State Guard, a Confederate force now led by former Missouri Governor Sterling Price. Lane had no intention of engaging Price's men in battle. His plan was to punish and wreak havoc in the towns where Price had been and which had provided provisions to the rebels during their march south. Lane had this to say about his motive for entering Missouri:

> . . . our sole mission is to play hell with Missouri. Missourians are
> wolves, snakes, devils, and damn their souls, I want to see them cast
> into a burning hell! We believe in a war of extermination. I want
> to see every foot of ground in Jackson, Cass, and Bates Counties
> burned over, everything laid to waste." (Soodalter)

In the late summer and fall of 1861, Lane's Brigade, operating out of Fort Scott, Kansas, would regularly ride into Vernon and Bates County, stealing supplies, plundering valuables and burning farms. In other words, jayhawking. In response, the Confederate leadership would send troops to try and protect these counties from Lane's

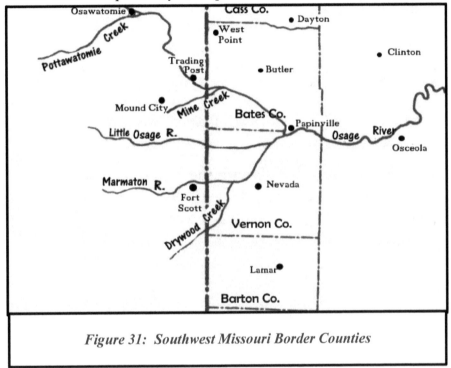

Figure 31: Southwest Missouri Border Counties

Brigade. Lane and his commanders did their best to avoid meeting up with the regular Confederate forces as they were generally outnumbered and large pitched battles were not the sort of battles in which Lane felt his Brigade would be victorious.

Even though Lane did not want to engage General Price's troops, his men under Charles Montgomery did meet up with the regular Confederate forces in Vernon County at Dry Wood Creek. The Battle of Dry Wood Creek occurred on September 2, 1861. The two armies met for a brief skirmish at which Lane's Brigade came away losers incurring five casualties. After this engagement, Lane sent a message to the War Department asking for reinforcements. This request was denied telling Lane that the troops were needed elsewhere and questioning his statement that southern Kansas was in danger. This denial angered Lane and he went on a rampage in western Missouri, leaving a path of destruction unlike anything seen up to this point in the

Civil War and one that would be compared to Sherman's March to the Sea in 1864. The result of Lane's trail of terror, which would continue into early 1862, would be a "wholesale rush of Missourians into the arms of the Confederacy" (Rafiner 128).

After suffering minimal losses at Dry Wood Creek, Lane's Brigade would relocate to West Point, a small town on the Missouri side of the border. From West Point, Lane would send Montgomery to Morristown after receiving news of a Confederate recruiting station in that town. The Morristown Raid would be the first time that Jayhawkers, would burn most of the buildings in the town to the ground. Before this, one or two selected buildings might be burnt, but not the entire town. After Morristown, this pattern of "total destruction" would become the norm

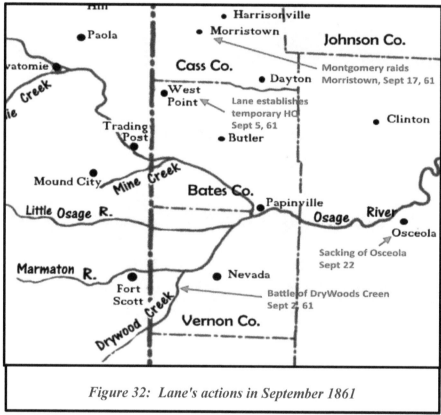

Figure 32: Lane's actions in September 1861

(Bisel 129). Two days after destroying Morristown, Lane's Brigade, again led by Montgomery, would leave West Point and head to Osceola, a small river town in St. Clair County. Here it was rumored that large stores of supplies were waiting for Confederate General Price and his men. Lane's Brigade and his men would destroy Papinville before arriving in Osceola on September 22, 1861.

Osceola was a town of 2,500 residents located at the junction of the Osage and the Sac Rivers. (the town is now located on the south side of Truman Lake which did not exist in 1861). Lane's men took anything of value in the city and loaded it in the wagons that they had conveniently brought with them. Lane's men reportedly stole over 300 horses and freed some 200 slaves. Lane's Brigade also helped themselves to a large store of whiskey. Many of his men had to be loaded into the wagons due to being too intoxicated to ride out of town. All but a small

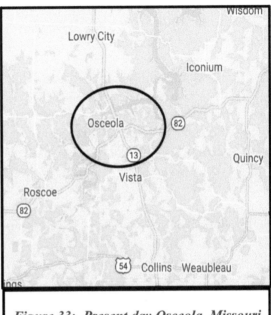

Figure 33: Present day Osceola, Missouri

number of the buildings in the town were burned including the courthouse. Some accounts say that Lane also had twelve citizens rounded up and shot. There is no definitive proof that this happened. This report is likely confusing this raid with the Morristown Raid where this did happen. Regardless, it is agreed that fifteen to twenty citizens likely were killed during this raid. (Soodalter)

The reports concerning the raid on Osceola vary greatly depending on the source you are reading. Reading northern newspapers you might think that Lane and his men walked old ladies across the street and taught Bible school classes. The southern reports of the same event may lead you to believe that Lane was the devil himself, his men drunks and criminals who were perpetrating this horrendous act on this innocent village. Americans on both sides of the war were shocked and outraged by Lane's actions. Kansas Governor Robinson was incensed, as was Union General Henry Halleck, Commander of the Department of Missouri, who said this of Lane and his men:

They are no better than a band of robbers; they cross the line, rob, steal, plunder, and burn whatever they can lay their hands upon. They disgrace the name and uniform of American soldiers. . . . The course pursued by those under Lane, has turned against us many thousands who were formerly Union men. A few more raids will make this state as unanimous against us as is Eastern Virginia (Goodrich, Black Flag 26)

President Lincoln, Lane's friend, did not punish Lane. He conveniently chose not to address the issue. He took no official stance saying that he preferred generals who took action as opposed to those who did nothing. "Remember Osceola" was a battle cry used two years later at the raid of Lawrence by William Quantrill's raiders in 1863. (Rulen.com)

Prior to the raid, Osceola was a thriving town of 2,500 residents; after the raid, only 200 people remained. The town has never fully

---

Burning of Osceola Monument

<u>Inscription Reads:</u>

In June 1861, President Abraham Lincoln issued an order making the U.S. Senator from Kansas, James H. Lane, a Brigadier General.

In September 1861, Gen. Lane and his rabble army of Kansas Jayhawkers, under questionable authority from Mr. Lincoln, invaded Missouri. His objective was to pillage and destroy peaceable, prosperous Osceola.

On September 21st, & 22nd, the Jayhawkers invaded, occupied, sacked and torched Osceola. Twelve male citizens sought to protect one of the banks from being looted and ultimately burned. Gen. Lane arrested these citizens for "treason" and, by way of a "drumhead court-martial", appointed himself prosecutor and judge, condemning the twelve to death.

He mustered a makeshift firing squad, in which he himself took part, murdering all but three of the twelve men, thinking they were all dead.

Figure 34: The Burning of Osceola Monument. Located in Osceola Cemetery, State Highway WW, Osceola, Missouri

recovered from this event. As of 2020, only 900 people call Osceola home. In September of 2011, on the 150th anniversary of the raid, the Osceola Board of Aldermen passed a resolution formally asking the University of Kansas to stop using the Jayhawk as their mascot due to the death and destruction that the name conjures in the minds of Osceolans. The University did not respond to the request.

Returning from Osceola, the raiders would continue their pillaging and burning of towns and farms on their journey back to their temporary headquarters at West Point. The residents of Bates County would watch as "Pianos, silk dresses and all manner of personal property left Missouri for Kansas homes and markets. (Rafiner 133). "Columns of liberated slaves as well as horses and mules" also followed Lane's Brigade back to Kansas.

After Osceola, Lane and his command would be ordered to Kansas City for a few weeks after which they would head south again. They would stop in Pleasant Hill for a couple of days and then march to Springfield, leaving a path of burned and looted farms and towns in their wake. Along the way, the towns of Rose Hill, Kingsville, Clinton, Butler, Humansville, Springfield and Lamar would all feel the wrath of Lane's war against Missouri.

It would be on this final leg of Lane's Missouri tour that Union generals would begin to question Lane's tactics and his ability to control his men. General David Hunter would question these things, in addition, to publicly questioning Lane's honesty. Lane would also have a verbal confrontation with General Samuel Sturgis in Bolivar, Missouri where Lane maintained that his men did not engage in theft. General Sturgis disagreed.

Unfortunately for Lane, in early November, his nemesis, General Hunter was named Commander of the Department of the West. He immediately ordered Lane and his men back to Fort

Figure 35: General David Hunter, Commander of the Department of the West

Scott. On the journey to Fort Scott, Lane's Brigade stayed true to their ways, stealing and burning the entire way back. A member of the brigade recalled it this way:

> *On our journey back, we spread havoc for miles on either side, taking negroes, mules, wagons, carriages, and horses until every soldier had a least two or three head of horses. We were breaking the law, not only of Missouri, but of the Federal Government (Fry 86).*

In all, before arriving back at Fort Scott on November 15th, Lane's Brigade had been in Missouri for 76 days. They had covered over 400 miles and had plundered and burned between 1,600 and 2,400 Missouri farms (Rafiner 142). They also left thousands of Missouri residents destitute and homeless with winter coming soon.   How many Missourians lost their lives is hard to say as one of Lane's practices was to have prisoners dig their own graves before ordering his men to carry out the execution. Historian Don Gilmore described the state of western Missouri in this way,

> *The Jayhawkers had become a pox, and everywhere they traveled or stopped, for a radius of several miles in every direction, the area became blighted or despoiled. The people, whether living in town or in the country, now lived in a state of continual terror (149).*

Shortly after arriving back in Fort Scott and with his enemy General Hunter now taking over the Department of the West, Lane would leave his command and go back to Washington to don his other hat, that of a U.S. Senator. Meanwhile back in Kansas, Governor Robinson, in conjunction with General Hunter, would be taking steps to reduce the impact that Lane could have as a military leader. Lane would spend his time in Washington trying to garner more power.   He would use his relationship with President Lincoln and stories about the success of Lane's Brigade to attempt to gain approval for a plan he concocted called "Lane's Expedition" which was to be an invasion through Arkansas and down into Texas by a large force commanded by Lane himself. In the end, Lincoln sided with Hunter and told Lane that Hunter was in command and that Lane reported to him and would follow the orders given by his commander.

Charles "Doc" Jennison was born in New York and briefly practiced medicine and preached abolition in Wisconsin before moving his family to Osawatomie, Kansas in 1857, at the age of 23. It is suspected, but not documented, that Jennison met fellow Osawatomie resident and abolitionist, John Brown, during his brief time in Osawatomie. Jennison followed Brown's almost fanatical opposition to the practice of slavery and those who supported it. Jennison would relocate to Mound City, Kansas, later that same year, where he quickly became involved in the local politics of Mound City. When he arrived in town there was a dispute with Paris, a nearby town, as to which town would be the county seat of Linn County.

At the time, Paris was the unofficial county seat, but voters chose Mound City to be the new county seat. Upset by the election results, the citizens of Paris threatened to contest the election. In

Figure 36: Mound City, Kansas. Where "Doc" Jennison began his vigilante career. Paris, Kansas, no longer exists

response to this threat, Jennison recruited a group of men and rode into Paris where he and his men gathered up all the county records, loaded them into wagons, and took them back to Mound City, which remains the county seat today.

Jennison started border raiding as part of the group that rode with another notable Jayhawker, James Montgomery. While briefly riding with Montgomery, Jennison began his career by making quick scavenging trips across the border into Missouri. At the time, it was not important which state someone lived in, as Jennison would terrorize all pro-slavery settlers, regardless of whether they were in Missouri or Kansas. It didn't take Jennison long to tire of Montgomery's "moral code of conduct" and he quickly broke away from Montgomery's unit, taking some of the more radical, "less moral" riders with him.

It is believed that the term "Jayhawker" was originally used to describe Charles "Doc" Jennison and his men. The actions of Jennison and his Jayhawkers laid the groundwork for the negative context that came with the term Jayhawk. Jennison and his men were all about plunder and making pro-slavery settlers pay for their support of the immoral institution of slavery.

Figure 37: James Montgomery, Image courtesy of Kansas Historical Society

The first documented action by Jennison and his vigilante militia occurred in November of 1860, when his men acted as judge, jury and executioner of Russell Hinds for working as a slave hunter. During a raid on pro-slavery settlers living near Trading Post, Kansas, Jennison rounded up all the pro-slavery men in the community and held a trial for them. Even though the men were found to be guilty of supporting slavery, they were all released except Russell Hinds. The men, other than Hinds, were told that they would be released if they left Kansas immediately. Hinds was a known slave hunter who would capture fugitive slaves and then return them to Missouri for five dollars a head. In Jennison's mind, slave hunters were the lowest of the low. Jennison sent out a warning to all slave owners and slave hunters when, after hanging Hinds, he left a note in his coat pocket which read. "This man was executed by the [citizens] of Kansas for being engaged in the hunting of Negroes in 1859. November 11, 1860. P.S. As all others will be that is found in the same occupation" (Rafiner 111).

After murdering Hinds, Jennison wrote a letter to George L. Stearns, where he described slave hunters as follows:

> . . . *for the last year that this county has been infested by a band of desperadoes known as Kidnapers [sic] and that it has become necessary for us as Anti-Slavery Men to take a stand against that and accordingly as the offences [sic] become more frequent we resolved and publickly [sic] two [sic] that any man found guilty of that crime should pay the forfeit with his life and accordingly as we had the proof we arrested one Rus Hinds and tried him publicly and hung him for being engaged [sic] in that unholy business....."* (Titterington)

Figure 38: Charles "Doc" Jennison

Jennison and his men would follow up the killing of Hinds with the execution of four Kansas men by the end of November 1860. Their crime? Being pro-slavery men.

The territorial government of Kansas could not abide this lawlessness and vigilantism being perpetrated by Jennison in the name of anti-slavery and they labeled him an outlaw. Kansas officials offered a reward and sent Captain Nathaniel Lyon and two companies of federal regulars to Mound City, in December of 1860, to capture him and James Montgomery. When they arrived, both men were nowhere to be found, having already been warned by anti-slavery friends at higher levels. Jennison spent the next few months as a wanted man but the firing on Fort Sumter in April of 1861, would change that status.

It's important to note that up to this point, Jennison was acting on his own with no official status. The onset of the Civil War changed this. Kansas Governor Robinson decided that Kansas needed men with Jennison's particular skills. To that end, all his crimes were forgiven, and Robinson gave Jennison a Colonel's commission and tasked him, under the leadership of Jim Lane, with raising the Seventh Kansas Volunteer Cavalry. Robinson had essentially assigned the fox to guard the hen house.

The 7th Volunteer Cavalry, often called Jennison's

Figure 39: "Doc" Jennison

Figure 40: William Cody at age 19 and later as Buffalo Bill Cody

Jayhawkers, or the Independent Mounted Kansas Jayhawkers, would be a part of Lane's Brigade and would go on to establish quite a reputation throughout the country. One historian contends that "no other regiment in the Union Army had so bad a reputation" (Etchesen). It's not surprising that the regiment had such a reputation when one looks at some of the notable members of the unit. Daniel Read Anthony, a Leavenworth, Kansas newspaperman and the brother of women's suffrage advocate Susan B Anthony, served as a leader of one of the companies and second in command to Jennison of the entire 7th Kansas Cavalry. Anthony would become known for his brutality in leading several raids in Missouri during the winter of 1861. Marshall Cleveland, a captain in company H was a known outlaw. William Cody, later known as Buffalo Bill Cody, was at this point a 16-year-old horse thief. John Brown Jr, son of and follower of his noted abolitionist father was the commander of Company K.

While officially Jennison's 7th Kansas Cavalry was part of Lane's Brigade, Jennison operated almost entirely independently of any leadership from Lane or any other higher authority. Jennison and his principal lieutenant, Daniel Anthony would inflict death and destruction upon the western Missouri counties far worse than Lane's earlier foray into Missouri. It should be noted that some of the worst acts by Jennison's 7th Cavalry were committed while Anthony was in charge and Jennison was actually back in Squiresville, a Kansas town just across the border that served as sort of a home base for Jennison's unit. Jennison, a frequent gambler, is said to have spent much of

Figure 41: Daniel Read Anthony, 2nd in command of the Kansas, a newspaper editor and brother of Susan B. Anthony.

his time in Squiresville playing cards. The winter of 1861 – 1862, with Anthony leading the men, would prove to be one of the most destructive and vicious periods of destruction during the entire war.

It would be Anthony who would lead the men into Independence, Missouri, a town just east of Kansas City on November 14, 1861. While in Independence, Anthony corralled all the local men in the public square where he divided them up into Union men and Southern Sympathizers. The Union men were released with their belongings. The rebels were then forced to listen to Anthony preach to them for hours about their evil ways. The Southern men were eventually released after all their belongings were taken from them. Several residents of Independence, who were off fighting for the Union in the Civil War, would have their stores looted and their homes and businesses burned to the ground. The Seventh Kansas Cavalry left the city with 70 horses, 20 wagons and 50 negroes (White Cloud 2).

Major General Henry W. Halleck, the Commander of the Department of Missouri, called Jennison's unit "no better than a band of robbers" and harshly criticized Jennison for "crossing the line to rob, steal, plunder and burn whatever they could lay their hands on." He wrote to General George McClellen:

> *The conduct of the forces under Lane and Jennison has done more for the enemy in this State than could have been accomplished by 20,000 of his own army. I receive almost daily complaints of outrages committed by these men in the name of the United States, and the evidence is so conclusive as to leave no doubt of their correctness. (Titterington)*

Colonel Frederick Steele, the commander of the Union forces in Sedalia Missouri had this to say about Jennison and his men:

> *They disgrace the name and uniform of American soldiers and are driving good Union men into the ranks of the secession army. Their conduct within the last six months has caused a change of 20,000 votes in this State. If the Government countenances such acts by screening the perpetrators from justice and by rewarding with office their leaders and abettors, it may resign all hopes of pacification of Missouri. If Kansas troops are again permitted to come into this State to commit depredations, the State can be held only by the strong arm of military power. The bitter animosity created against these troops is naturally transferred to the Government which supports them, and, in whose name, they pretend to act. (Titterington)*

While traveling through Jackson and Cass County, Anthony and Jennison would burn everything in their path, regardless of the politics of the homeowner. Jennison made a point to call his command a "self-sustaining Army" and with that in mind, they took everything of any value from each home that they passed. This included food, clothing, money, jewelry, furniture, livestock, horses and slaves. The policy of taking slaves was problematic because slavery was still legal in the state of Missouri and many Union supporters owned slaves at the time. The official Union Army policy was that slaves were not to be freed through military action. The Seventh simply ignored the policy and freed all slaves they encountered. This is another instance of a situation where Union supporters were converted to Confederate sympathizers since they saw this as the only way to protect their property. One future guerilla relates this story of his father confronting Doc Jennison and telling him that he was and always had been a strong Union man and that his home should not be destroyed. In response to this man's pleas, Jennison replied:

You are just like all of these damn Missourians. You claim to be strong Union men when we are around, but as soon as we are gone, you are secesh. We are going to take everything that we want in spite of your claims" (Gilmore, Black Flag 35).

In the winter of 1861, Anthony went as far as to set up a winter camp in Morristown. If you recall, Morristown had already been raided and burned down twice prior to the winter of 1861. To western Missouri residents this "permanent camp" meant that instead of worrying about the Kansas troops only when they happened to be passing by, they had to worry about them all the time. In effect, this meant that Anthony and the 7th would be regular visitors to every farm in the area to ensure that the men in his "self-sustaining army" were provided for during the winter months (Rafiner 154).

Anthony chose Morristown as his base of operations for the winter because it was very close to the Kansas border and was a good place to store stolen goods and cattle before taking them back to Kansas where they would be sold at auction. Much of the stolen cattle were sold in Squiresville, while other goods would be transported to Lawrence, which had become a destination for most of the goods that had been stolen from Missouri. Lucian Carr, a writer and Kansas abolitionist called Lawrence, "a mere fence-house for stolen property from Missouri captured by Jayhawkers and Red Legs." The central clearinghouse for goods stolen from Missouri was the Johnson House Hotel on Vermont Street in Lawrence. Across from the hotel, there was a ravine in which crude structures were built using straw bales. These straw warehouses were piled high with stolen goods from Missouri and the residents of Lawrence and its surrounding area had no qualms about purchasing these stolen goods at regularly held auctions (Gilmore, Red Legs 7).

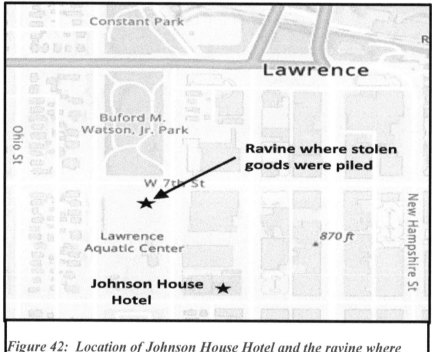

Figure 42: Location of Johnson House Hotel and the ravine where stolen goods were stored prior to being auctioned in regular sales

From their base in Morristown, Anthony and Jennison would carry out several raids during which the towns attacked were completely or partially destroyed. The raided towns would include Harrisonville, Pleasant Hill, Dayton, Columbus, West Point and southern Jackson County. The small hamlet of Dayton would be the location of a particularly brutal attack on January 1st, 1862. Anthony and his men would burn all but one of the 49 buildings to the ground. Three Dayton men were also arrested, tried, found guilty and executed during this raid. The result of this raid was that every resident of Dayton, which included over 40 families, had no shelter during a particularly harsh winter. It was not only the people who lived in the attacked towns that faced the harsh reality of winter without shelter. The trails to and from the devastated towns would be littered with a line of pillaged and burned homes and farms.

Around Kingsville, a small town just southeast of Pleasant Hill in western Johnson County, Missouri, an eyewitness recalls, "I counted

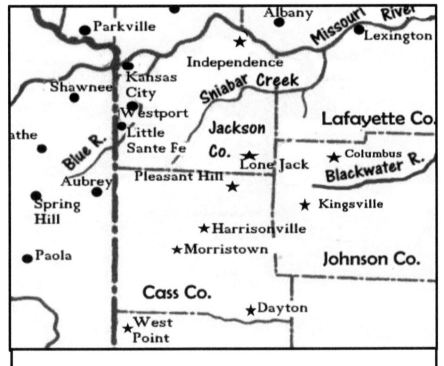

Figure 43: Stars show towns that were destroyed or partially destroyed by the 7th Kansas Cavalry in the winter of 1861-1862

one evening, while standing on Brushy Knob, one hundred and sixty houses on fire." During the Kingsville raid, which happened one week after Dayton on January 9th, eight men were executed (Goodrich 24).

The 7th Kansas Cavalry would leave their winter camp at Morristown in early February of 1862. Before their departure, the soldiers had spent a great deal of time in southern Jackson county stealing anything of value, livestock and slaves. As the Kansans left the camp at Morristown, it is said that the wagon train of valuables and other stolen property was "four to five miles long" (Miller 75). This wagon train of stolen Missouri property would go back to Kansas where they would be sold in the auctions at Squiresville and Lawrence to the highest bidder. William Cody, aka Buffalo Bill, described the raids that he participated in as a Jayhawker this way, "Few of us ever returned empty-handed . . . We were the biggest gang of thieves on record" (Gilmore, Red Legs 14). Nobody was happy with the actions of the 7th Kansas Cavalry under Doc Jennison. Missouri Unionist politician and artist George Caleb Bingham summed it up this way, "If Jennison were hung, [Confederate] General Sterling Price would lose the best recruiting agent he ever had" (Everything Ablaze).

Despite the criticism from Halleck, Steele and others, Jennison was promoted by Major General David Hunter to Brigadier General in January of 1862. In a strange about-face, five days later, General Hunter issued Order Number 17 in the Department of Kansas, which basically installed martial law in the area to stop the practice of jayhawking by Jennison and others. The order made jayhawking a crime that would be dealt with by military courts.

Figure 44: Jemison's [sic] Jayhawkers. This 1864 etching shows a Missouri farm and woman being attacked by a Jayhawker. Image courtesy of the Library of Congress

General Halleck, never a fan of Jennison, attempted to move Jennison and his men away from the Missouri/Kansas border by issuing orders in April 1862, for Jennison and the Seventh to report to New

Mexico to fight the Apache. This order, along with being passed over for a promotion, infuriated Jennison and he promptly resigned his commission. He made speeches to his men calling the current military leaders "pro-slavery" and urging his men to follow him and resign from service. For these speeches, Jennison was arrested and held in a military prison in St. Louis in the spring and summer of 1862. Jennison's popularity in Kansas was a problem for the military. He was soon released without a trial and returned to Kansas where he was hailed as an anti-slavery hero. For the next eighteen months or so, Jennison retired to civilian life, although it was widely rumored that during this retirement, he led a band of Red Legs on many Missouri raids.

Figure 45: A Red Leg is featured in "Evacuation of Missouri Counties Under Order Number 11", by George Caleb Bingham, 1870. Image courtesy of the State Historical Society of Missouri, Art Collection

The Red Legs are an interesting study during this period. The term Red Legs is often used as a general term that is synonymous with Jayhawkers, but this is not correct. The Red Legs were a group that was separate and distinct from other Jayhawkers. In plain terms, Red Legs were all Jayhawkers, but Jayhawkers were not all Red Legs. At its core, the term Red Legs refers to the red leggings that were worn by the men who rode under this name. These red leggings can be seen worn by the central character in the famous George Caleb Bingham painting, Martial Law, shown in Figure 44. There is much controversy in historical circles as to who these men were, how the group or groups got started, and whether the groups were functioning as part of the Union army or whether they were just men lured by the idea of easy money like other Jayhawkers.

There is little doubt that the original Red Legs worked as scouts for the Union Army. These men were often the "best of the best" in terms of their skills at tracking, fighting, shooting and riding. You might think of them as the Border War's version of today's Navy Seals or Army Rangers. There is very little information available concerning the activities of the Red Legs and what it was like to ride with them. Compare this to large amounts of newspaper reports, letters and other documents that were created by the regular Jayhawker bands. It's almost as if the Red Legs took an oath of secrecy. One might compare their clandestine operations much the way we think of the CIA today.

Figure 46: William Sloan Tough; Blunt's Chief of Scouts and known Red Leg leader

My research leads me to believe that it is likely some of the Red Legs, who originally worked for and were paid by the Union Army, eventually left their employ, but gathered together to go into Missouri and prosper through jayhawking activities. General James Blunt, then the Commander of the District of Kansas, called out the Red Legs in a communication to one of his commanders when he said:

Red Legs, which is an organized band of thieves and violators of law and good order. All persons found prowling the country, without a legitimate purpose, must be disarmed; and if they shall be caught in the act of thieving or other such lawlessness, or in the possession of stolen property, for which they cannot give a good and sufficient reason, they shall be shot upon the spot! (Gilmore, Red Legs 10)

Some historians believe this statement by General Blunt was simply a ruse for his superiors. He was saying the right things to make it look like he was taking steps to stop groups like the Red Legs from wreaking havoc across the countryside. However, his statement loses some of its impact when we learn from Thomas J Anderson of Topeka, a former member of Blunt's staff, that "Blunt had many [Red Legs] on his staff," and also "had many of them on the payroll" (Gilmore, Red Legs 11). It is known that one of the leaders of the Red Legs was William Sloan Tough, who just happened to be Blunt's Chief of Scouts.

Were the Red Legs directed by Blunt and therefore the Union Army, or were they just skilled men who decided to go off on their own and use the war to make themselves rich? Blunt maintained throughout his life that he had nothing do with the Red Legs who participated in jayhawking and there is no hard proof to say otherwise. We will likely never know for sure. What we do know is that a Red Leg unit of 30 – 100 men sprang up in Kansas about the same time that Charles "Doc" Jennison was supposedly retiring to civilian life after being released from his St. Louis prison in 1862. Coincidence? To the common citizens of the time, the terms "Jayhawkers" and "Red Legs" became synonymous.

William "Bloody Bill" Anderson was the son of a wealthy, pro-slavery landowner in Council Grove, Kansas. The Anderson family, who did not own any slaves, also ran a grocery store and a commodities business that sold to travelers on the Sante Fe trail. The life of a merchant was not for William and in 1860, he and his brother Jim, would begin stealing horses

Figure 47: William "Bloody Bill" Anderson wearing a guerrilla shirt

in Missouri and then bringing them back across the border to Kansas, where he would sell them.

In May 1862, an arrest warrant was issued for one of Anderson's cohorts in the horse-stealing business. Anderson's father was infuriated by the warrant as it had been issued by Judge Baker, a man who had been a friend of the Anderson family. With a pistol in hand and bad intentions in mind, the elder Anderson went to the Council Grove courthouse to confront Judge Baker. Upon arrival at the courthouse, the elder Anderson was restrained by a constable and eventually shot by Judge Baker in the scuffle that took place. Young William, 22-years-old at the time, was enraged by the death of his father and further infuriated when he found out that Judge Baker would not be charged with murder, as the authorities determined the shooting to be in self-defense. Anderson vowed to get revenge for his father's death.

William, who now had a warrant out for his arrest for hiding the cohort for whom the original warrant was issued, took his three sisters and moved them to Westport, Missouri. A short month later in June of 1862, William and his brother Jim returned to Council Grove to confront Judge Baker. After luring the judge and his brother-in-law into a store, the Anderson brothers ambushed them, trapping them in the basement of the store. Barricading the door, the Anderson brothers lit the store on fire and watched as the two captives were burned to death in the fire.

Figure 48: William T. Anderson, aka "Bloody Bill" Anderson. Image courtesy of the Library of Congress

Shortly after the murder, Anderson and another man with whom he had been riding, were arrested and charged with murder in Olathe, Kansas. Both men were tried, convicted and sentenced to death by a 12-man jury. Fortunately for Anderson, the authorities in town could not find any volunteers who were willing to assist in Anderson's execution. The sheriff decided to take him to Leavenworth to be executed but Anderson escaped during that trip and rode back to Missouri. Anderson is said to have announced before leaving Olathe, "Gentlemen, I will visit your town again" (Blair 114).

William was a hard man and never even pretended to care from whom he stole. He told one friend, "I don't care anymore than you for the South . . .. but there is a lot of money in this business" (Erwin 57). Anderson would meet up with Quantrill in 1863 after Quantrill scolded him and his small group of thieves for stealing from Southern Sympathizers. Apparently impressed by Quantrill, Anderson would join his band of raiders shortly thereafter. This scolding by Quantrill is thought to have stuck with Anderson and possibly been a reason for issues between the two men later in the war. Anderson was not with Quantrill during the raid of Olathe but was a central figure in the Quantrill story. Several of the bloodier acts attributed to Quantrill and his men can be traced back to Bloody Bill.

George Todd, Bushwhacker

George Todd was born in Montreal but moved with his family to Missouri when he was a very young man. A stonemason and bridge builder with his father before the war, Todd joined the Missouri State Militia when the war first started, but left the organized unit in early 1862, when he joined up with Quantrill's Bushwhackers.

Riding with Quantrill, Todd made a name for himself at the First Battle of Independence on August 11th, when he rescued several prisoners from the Independence jail. He also executed a pair of Union men who were known to have participated in several raids on Quantrill's men in the past. Only twenty-two years old when he joined Quantrill, Todd would rise in the ranks to become one of Quantrill's most trusted lieutenants.

Figure 49: George M. Todd, Image was taken between 1860 and 1862

Todd was described as "being crude, illiterate, hot-tempered, callously brutal, a deadly shot, and uncontrollable when drunk, his personal bravery and thirst for action were unquestionable" (McGregor). Four years younger than Quantrill, Todd was very popular with the younger riders many of whom would eventually follow him when he left Quantrill's command later in the war. Unlike many of his Bushwhacker brothers, Todd didn't seem to care if history justified his actions by considering him a soldier in the Confederate army. He declared, "You need not consider me a Confederate officer. I intend to follow bushwhacking as long as I live" (Erwin 58).

Todd gained quite a reputation in the border country during the first several years of the war. Newspaper reports during the era say that:

[Todd] was the incarnate devil of battle. He thought of fighting when awake, dreamed of it at night, mingled talk of it in relaxation, and went hungry many a day and went shelterless many a night that he might find his enemy and have his fill of fight. Quantrill always had to hold him back, and yet he was his thunderbolt. (Peterson 79)

William Clarke Quantrill

The greatest fault in the people who write of us is that they only tell one side of the story, just as though they [Redlegs, Jayhawkers and Yankee troops] had the right to murder, burn, rob and steal and those whom they murdered, robbed and plundered had no right to resist.
-William H Gregg, Quantrill Lieutenant, 1906

The central character of this manuscript and the leader of the Olathe Raid in 1862, is a 25-year-old schoolteacher, farmer, soldier and teamster named William Clarke Quantrill. It is necessary, when writing about Quantrill, to understand the sources of information from which history has formed its opinions of the man. Today's view of Quantrill is largely shaped by multiple biographies that have been written about him since his death. Several of these biographies seem to have "picked a side" in how they chose to portray Quantrill. He is either the devil or the hero. In the interest of brevity, this work will not provide a detailed analysis of each written account of Quantrill and his life. The reader, if interested, is encouraged to dig deeper into how the modern opinion of the man was formed by reviewing some of the many Quantrill books that are listed in the bibliography. In addition, there have been numerous newspaper and magazine stories written about William Quantrill that have been reviewed in the research for this work. The titles of these sources can also be found in the bibliography.

There have been several films that feature Quantrill as a main character in their story. Quantrill is a lead character in the 1940, John Wayne film titled, **Dark Command** and in the 1950, Audie Murphy film, **Kansas Raiders**. For those of us who love western films, these are good movies, but make no effort to stick to facts of the Border War or the life of William Quantrill. One of the most comical things about these early films is the lack of attention to detail regarding the age of the principal characters or the geographic topography of the Kansas border area. In **Kansas Raiders**, for example, the characters ride out of Lawrence, Kansas, and we see the mountains of the actual filming location of the Senora Desert in Arizona in the background. I'm not sure how many readers have been to Lawrence, Kansas, but I assure you, there are no mountains around Lawrence.

Many of the films also cast actors who are much older than Quantrill would have been at the time. Quantrill would have been in his mid-twenties during the height of his fame. Most films portray him as a man in his late thirties or forties. More historically accurate movies regarding the Border War era, but in which Quantrill is not a major character, are the more recent **Ride with the Devil** (1999) and **The Outlaw Josey Wales** (1976). These movies, while fictional and not specifically about Quantrill, do a better job of showing the mood of the border region during this tumultuous time. The bottom line is, if you are looking for historically accurate films about Quantrill, you will need to find a documentary rather than a Hollywood movie.

One final point to be made before delving into the life of William Quantrill is the controversy over the spelling of his name. Is it Quantrell or is it Quantrill? One possible explanation for the genesis of this confusion is provided by the "The Missouri Partisan Ranger" website, which attributes one possible explanation to a Mr. George Shepherd. Mr. Shepherd has uncovered a story about a young girl from Higginsville, Missouri, who made a flag with the name spelled incorrectly. While the flag made by Ms. Fickle may have been given to Quantrill, it is unlikely that they displayed it while going into battle as Quantrill and his men were generally disguised as Union soldiers.

Annie Fickle was 20-years-old when her home was invaded by federal soldiers. She was reportedly arrested, and then later rescued by a band of partisan soldiers. In payment for their kindness, Annie created a black flag with the word "QUANTRELL" horizontally printed across the flag in red letters. She then went to Quantrill's camp and presented the flag to Quantrill and his men. Quantrill is said to have taken the flag with him when he left Missouri for Kentucky in 1864 (Rulen.com). The actual flag has never been found and there is likely no way to determine if this story is true. What we do know is that newspapers writing about Quantrill during this time continually misspelled his name. The correct spelling of the name is "Quantrill". We know this, as we have family records provided by his mother, and multiple letters from Quantrill himself, to his mother, in which he signs his name, spelling it "Quantrill".

It is interesting to see all the different spellings that were used by newspapers of the period. In our modern world, a misspelling of a key name by a journalist would be an unacceptable mistake, but in the Civil

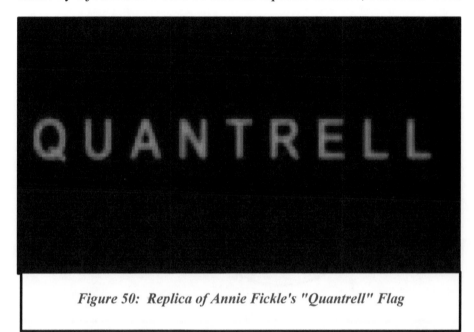

Figure 50: Replica of Annie Fickle's "Quantrell" Flag

War era, it was commonplace. There was no internet at the time to verify things like spelling. Many of the sources cited from that period were likely lone newspaper men, who not only wrote the stories but also printed and sold the newspapers themselves. Many of the newspapers at this time simply reprinted stories from other newspapers which meant that a misspelling, or even a factual error, would be propagated from one paper to another. Eventually, that error would be deemed to be fact, simply due to the number of sources that had reported it in a certain manner. In researching old newspaper accounts, one will often see the same language and descriptions used in multiple stories due to this practice of "reprinting" from another source.

William Clarke Quantrill was born in Canal Dover, Ohio, on July 31, 1837. Quantrill was the oldest of twelve children, four of which died in infancy, born to Thomas Quantrill and Caroline Cornelia Clarke Quantrill. The Quantrill family included its share of men of questionable character. William's uncle was a known pirate and his grandfather a gambler and horse trader. What the Quantrill men seemed to lack in integrity, they made up for in charisma, which allowed them to avoid serious consequences for their deeds.

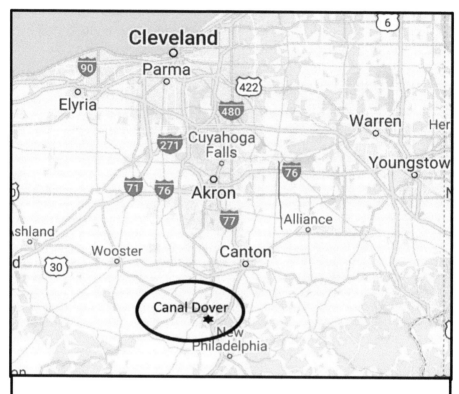

Figure 51: The birthplace of William Quantrill, Canal Dover, Ohio. now known as "Dover".

This charisma was evident in his father Thomas who, as a trustee of a local school district, embezzled school funds for personal reasons and was caught red-handed. Vowing revenge on the man who reported his thievery, Harmon Beeson, Thomas confronted Beeson and missed with a shot attempting to kill his enemy. For this act, he was arrested and charged with attempted murder. Despite being under indictment, Thomas was able to convince the local school leaders to name him Headmaster of the school. A position he held until his death from tuberculosis, in 1854.

Very little is known about young William's childhood in Canal Dover, now known simply as "Dover". Throughout his relatively short life, Quantrill was very private regarding his formative years. It is likely that after achieving notoriety for his actions on the Kansas/Missouri border, he was conscious about shielding his mother and siblings from people seeking retribution for his actions. Most of the information that has come out about this period in his life paints him as an excellent student, but a loner who spent a great deal of time wandering the woods hunting for small game. At fourteen he is said to have been one of the best marksmen in the area (Peterson 5). There are also stories, collected after his death, that contend that he was a "juvenile monster" who enjoyed shooting pigs in the ears, pinning snakes to trees to torture them and stabbing horses and cows. Castel contends that these stories should be taken with a grain of salt, as they were gathered after Quantrill had already achieved infamy. It is likely that these stories have taken certain events and twisted them to make sure that they paint the expected picture of Quantrill as an animal. Castel further notes that the people of Canal Dover were likely not thrilled with the fame brought to their town by their hometown product (24).

Quantrill is said to have been a good-looking young man, tall for the time at just under 6 feet with very blond, almost white hair. The hair color is a surprise to most as the very few pictures and drawings of Quantrill seem to show him with darker hair. According to his first lieutenant William Gregg, his hair got a little darker as he aged but was still blond. His beard and mustache would come in with highlights of red mixed with the blond hair. Multiple acquaintances mention Quantrill's blue-gray eyes. Gregg says that Quantrill, "had the brightest, most remarkable eyes you would find in a lifetime" (Beilein 27). Frank James described Quantrill in this way:

> *I will never forget the first time I saw Quantrill. He was nearly six feet in height, rather thin, his hair and mustache was [sic] sandy and he was full of life and a jolly fellow. He had none of the air of the bravado or the desperado about him. We all loved him at first sight . . .. (Goodrich, Black Flag 35)*

After his father died in 1854, the family was left with large financial debts. His mother converted the family home to a boarding house and William became a schoolteacher at the age of sixteen to help pay the bills. After teaching for a few terms in Canal Dover, Quantrill left the family home in 1855 and moved to Mendota, Illinois. In Mendota, he worked as a teacher and later at a lumberyard with hopes of making more money to send home to his family. While in Mendota, he was reportedly involved in a scuffle that resulted in a man being killed. Quantrill claimed self-defense and was released but was asked by authorities to leave town.

After leaving Mendota, he headed back to Canal Dover, but only made it as far as Fort Wayne, Indiana, where he took another teaching post in the spring of 1856. Within a year, he was back in Canal Dover teaching at a different school and living in poverty with his mother. Having failed in his attempt to improve the family's financial situation, Quantrill longed for adventure and a way to help his family financially.

Figure 52: This image of Quantrill was taken in 1856, when he would have been 19 years old. The image was reportedly owned by Kate King, seen in the image on the right. King was Quantrill's girlfriend and later wife during his short adult life. Image courtesy of www.CanteyMyersCollection.com

Quantrill's opportunity for adventure came in February 1857. His mother worked out a deal with two Canal Dover men, Henry Torrey and Harmon Beeson, to accompany the men to Kansas to lay claim to property and establish family farms. This was the same Harmon Beeson who Quantrill's father had tried to kill. The agreement was that 19-year-old William would accompany Beeson, Torrey and Beeson's son, Richard, to the Kansas Territory and would work with the men. In return they would pay for and file a land claim for Quantrill, who could not file his own claim since he was still a minor at the time. Quantrill jumped at the opportunity. The four men left for Kansas where they would lay claim to parcels of land near the Marais des Cygnes River close to Stanton, Kansas. Beeson and Torrey paid $250 each for their claims and filed Quantrill's claim in addition to their own.

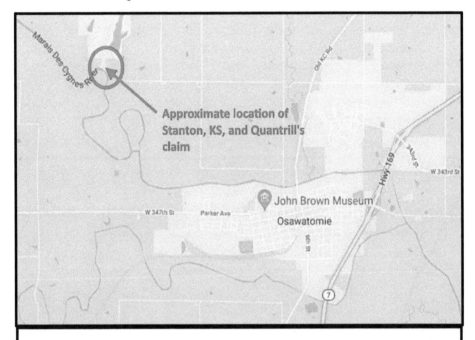

Figure 53: The exact location of the Beeson, Torrey, Quantrill claim is unknown, but records tell us that it was on the Marais Des Cygnes River, near Stanton, Kansas.

The four men worked and lived on the claims together in a one-room cabin on Torrey's farm. The work was hard and shared by all, with Quantrill reportedly doing much of the hunting to provide food for the group. By May 1857, cracks had begun to appear in the relationships and future partnership between the men. The initial plan was that Beeson and Torrey would provide the cash for Quantrill's claim. He would work it off, eventually paying his debt and take over the claim as his own. It appears that he may have come to mistrust the other men and doubt that he would ever get ownership of "his claim". In a letter to his mother, Quantrill tried to talk his mother into selling the home in Canal Dover and sending him the money so he could purchase another claim in the Kansas Territory.

Quantrill soon had a complete falling out with Beeson and Torrey and decided that the only way out was to sell his claim to his now-former partners. Unfortunately, the three men could not reach an agreement on how much should be paid to Quantrill for his claim. This argument came to a head when Quantrill took his complaint to the "squatter's mediation court". This was the agreed-upon way to handle property disputes in the Kansas Territory as there was no other system of civil law enforcement in the state at the time.

The squatter's court awarded Quantrill $63, to be paid by Beeson and Torrey in two payments. Unfortunately, the squatters' court lacked a way to enforce its judgments. Several sources say that the first payment was never made. Figure 54 seems to dispute that fact. My guess is that it was actually the second payment that was never made.

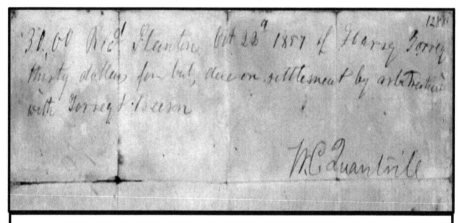

Figure 54: Receipt for the first $30 payment as ordered by the Squatters Court from Beeson and Torrey to Quantrill. Receipt reads "30.00 recd Stanton Oct 22, 1857 of Henry Torrey thirty dollars for but, due to settlement by arbitration with Torrey & Beeson" Signed by W.C. Quantrill. Image courtesy of Kansas Historical Society

When the "second payment" was not made, Quantrill went to the cabin and stole a yoke of oxen from Beeson and two pistols and a few blankets from Torrey.

Beeson was furious and soon confronted Quantrill. He put a gun to his head and forced him to give the oxen back. Quantrill would also return the guns to Torrey, but the blankets were never returned and were later found, beyond repair, stuffed into a rotten log. Despite this quarrel, Torrey and Quantrill remained friends, however, Beeson and Quantrill would never repair their relationship. In fact, Beeson was one of the main contributors to Connelley's extremely negative treatment of Quantrill in his book, *Quantrill and the Border Wars*. Torrey, on the other hand, always maintained kind words and feelings for Quantrill when asked about his friend in later years.

In late 1857, Beeson returned to Canal Dover to get the rest of his family and move them out to their new home in Kansas. His promising stories of the situation in Kansas is believed to have lured several other young men from Canal Dover to head to Kansas to start a new life. This group, consisting of mostly younger men, some of which were likely friends and acquaintances of Quantrill, laid claim to parcels of land in southern Johnson County, in a settlement called Tuscarora Lake or the Ohio Settlement.

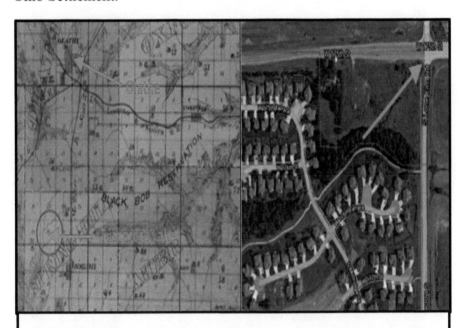

Figure 55: The map on the left shows the location of Tuscarora Lake in 1859. The image on the right show the same location today. The red arrow is pointing to the intersection of 175th Street and South Lone Elm Road. The lake, assuming there was one, no longer exists.

While living in Tuscarora Lake, Quantrill wrote a letter to a friend in which he made several comments which tell us that at this time he still maintained his "Northern view" of the world. In this letter, Quantrill commented that the "Lecompton Constitution which would make Kansas a slave state was a "swindle". He also wrote, "Jim Lane was as good a man as we have" and that two Missouri Southerners were recently killed in self-defense and it was a "shame that it was not more". Experiences and acquaintances would drastically change this Northern view over the next two years (Leslie 51).

Author William Connelley reports that while staying in Lake Tuscarora, Quantrill was caught stealing from the other members of the community. They reportedly asked him to leave the settlement, but there is no historical evidence to back up this charge of larceny. The fact that no charges were brought would lead one to believe that it could

Figure 56: This image shows Quantrill in 1859, at the age of 22. The image was taken in Colorado shortly after he left the Russell, Majors and Waddell Freighting Company. Image courtesy of www.canteymyerscollections.com

be an embellishment of some smaller infraction by Quantrill that has been amplified by the passage of time and the feelings regarding Quantrill in post-Civil War Kansas.

We do know that Quantrill would leave the Tuscarora settlement in January of 1858. Now twenty-years-old, Quantrill would become a bit of a nomad for the next two years. Fort Leavenworth would serve as his base at this time. From Leavenworth he took several jobs that would take him out west. He would work as a cattle driver, teamster, quartermaster's clerk and a cook, on these trips to the west. We know that he would make at least two trips west returning to Fort Leavenworth after the first to sign on for a second trip. On his return, he would stop in various mining towns to try his hand at gold mining and gambling.

Prior to the Civil War, government agents would use anyone that they could find to drive wagons to the west. The recruiting for these teamsters was mostly accomplished in saloons. Because Leavenworth was a pro-slavery town, most of the men in the saloons were pro-slavery, which meant that most of the men who were hired for the journeys that Quantrill made to the west followed that ideology. Remember that Quantrill, at this point in his life, was a twenty-one-year-old man who hadn't had a strong male figure in his life for the past several years. The fact that Quantrill spent all his time on these trips with these pro-slavery men, makes it easier to understand how his feelings about the issues of slavery could change.

It would be the summer of 1859 before Quantrill would arrive back in Kansas, having just completed a harrowing trip from Utah. The trip from Utah, which began with 19 men in the traveling party, would include spending time looking for gold on Pike's Peak, surviving multiple blizzards, snow blindness and Indian attacks. Only 12 of the 19 men who started from Utah would return to Kansas alive. Four years after he had left Canal Dover to seek his fortune, Quantrill arrived back in Kansas no better off financially than he had been when he left, and still searching for his life's purpose. He would eventually take a job teaching school in Stanton, Kansas, very near where he, Beeson and Torrey had originally settled two years prior.

In a letter to his mother in January of 1860, Quantrill would give us the first indication that his views on the question of slavery had changed. In this letter, he notes that while the newspapers talk about the bad things that the pro-slavery men had done, it was usually the abolitionists who had caused most of the problems. He went on to say that these abolitionist groups were made up of some of the "most lawless people in the country". His letter also mentions John Brown when he says that most abolitionists sympathize and look up to Brown, whom he calls "a murderer and a robber" who "should have been hung years ago" (Leslie 62). These private letters show a more accurate perspective of his political views even though publicly, and in his role as a schoolteacher, he continued to advocate for Kansas to be a free-state.

Once the school year ended in Stanton, Quantrill would go to Lawrence, where on a previous trip, he had befriended some Native Americans on the Delaware Reservation which was across the Kansas River, northeast of Lawrence. He would move into a small cabin on

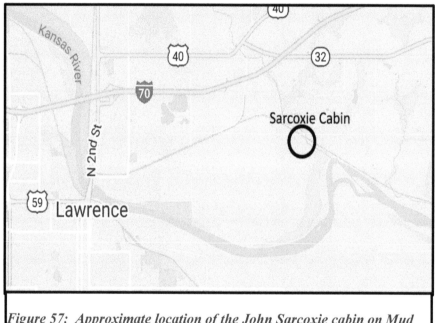

Figure 57: Approximate location of the John Sarcoxie cabin on Mud Creek

Mud Creek with his friend, John Sarcoxie, who was the son of a Delaware Chief. It was during this time, in late 1860, that Quantrill would meet the men who would influence him to pursue the path which would make his name live in infamy for generations to come.

It is important to note that between the fall of 1860 and December of 1861, all the history we have of Quantrill is provided by abolitionists from Kansas. Keep in mind, during this time on the border of Kansas and Missouri, there were two sides to every story and the heroes and villains in every story were very dependent on the political views of the person telling the story. That said, the sources providing information about Quantrill during this period were relatively trusted sources. These sources, while definitely having a "side", were not known for exaggeration in terms of the information that they had provided. Rather they were businessmen and other local men in authority positions mainly around the Lawrence area.

While living with Sarcoxie in the cabin on Mud Creek, Quantrill would make frequent trips to Lawrence where he would meet several men of "questionable character". These men would gather around the Kansas River ferry landing, which was located across the river from Lawrence. These men were border ruffians who would gather at the ferry to drink and roughhouse as well as listen and watch for "business oppor-tunities". These opportunities included chances to steal anything that they might be able to sell on either the Kansas or Missouri side of the border. They would often steal goods, guns, slaves, horses and cattle. The slaves would usually be taken to Missouri and sold back to their masters, while the rest of the "property" would be sold anywhere that a willing buyer could be found.

Figure 58: Quantrill was believed to have suffered from yellow fever in Lawrence in 1860. He was nursed by Lydia Stone, the daughter of a local hotel owner. After his recovery, Quantrill gave Lydia a ruby ring and this image of himself. The back of the case is inscribed, "To Lydia from Quantrill 1860". This writing is in Quantrill's hand. Image courtesy of www.canteymyerscollection.com

Figure 59: Image of Quantrill, taken in 1860. Reportedly was "Quantrill's favorite of himself". Quantrill suffered from granulated eyelids, which you can see in this image. Image courtesy of www.canteymyerscollection.com

Quantrill's new friends were mostly Missourians who held pro-slavery views, which may have solidified the viewpoint that Quantrill had taken on his trips out west with the proslavery teamsters. While hanging out with these men, Quantrill likely participated in several robberies of farms and homesteads in the border region. These men did not care what political views the resident had, they were in it for themselves and the bounty to be gained. Based on the company he was keeping; it is safe to say that it was likely during this period that Quantrill learned some of the skills that would serve him well in the next phase of his life. A phase that would include recruiting and commanding, arguably, the most notorious band of guerrillas to ever have existed in the United States.

On June 23, 1860, Quantrill would pen a letter to his mother, which would prove to be the last time anyone from Canal Dover would ever hear from him. In this letter, he talked about crops and asked his mother if she had received the money that he had previously sent. He wrote that he missed home and would be home in September of that year. A promise he would not keep. His mother would never hear from him again as he was apparently trying to put distance between his past and his new self. It was around this time that, while in Lawrence, he would begin using the name Charley Hart full time. Only a few of his closest friends knew his real name.

Why was he using an alias? We don't really know. One possibility might be that he knew he was going to be making his living outside the bounds of law and he didn't want to sully his reputation with his mother and family back in Canal Dover in case word of his criminal activity ever got back to them. Indeed, after the letter to his mother in June, he would never again, even on his deathbed, talk of being from Canal Dover, nor of his true family history. Another thought is that he was already thinking about crafting a new life history that would better support his intended path of criminal activity. We don't know the reason for this separation from his past. We do know that he went back to using William Quantrill at the height of his notoriety as the leader of Quantrill's raiders, which seems inconsistent with the reasons for the alias presented above.

When not hanging out with his bushwhacker friends on the dock, Quantrill would go into Lawrence, where he, aka Charley Hart, would claim he was employed as a Delaware Nation detective. In Lawrence, he would become friendly with prominent Jayhawkers such as Captain John E Stewart, "The Fighting Preacher". Stewart was an abolitionist Methodist Minister who was famous for helping slaves escape and providing a place for them to stay at Fort Stewart before he helped them

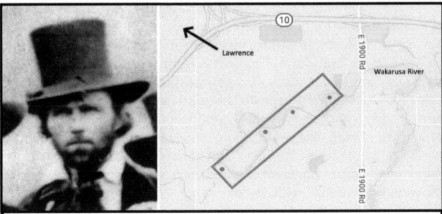

Figure 60: Reverend John E. Stewart, "The Fighting Preacher". The map shows possible locations of "Stewart's Fort" which was said to have been located approximately 4 miles SW of Lawrence on the south side of a horseshoe bend of the Wakarusa River.

make their way north. Fort Stewart was his well-protected homestead southwest of Lawrence on the Wakarusa River.

The John Stewart relationship is a good example of how Quantrill took great risks by playing both sides of the coin. The Fighting Preacher was not a man who was bound by the ten commandments and was known to have made a considerable amount of money profiting from various illegal activities. On one occasion Quantrill, with another cattle rustler, moved a large stolen herd of cattle toward Stewart's Fort on the Wakarusa River. Lawrence authorities were hot on their trail and when they arrived at the fort, Stewart, likely for a cut of the profits, swore that an unknown person had simply left the herd for a short time to let them rest. Shortly after being bailed out by Stewart, Quantrill would participate in an attack on "Stewart's Fort" to try and capture slaves so that they could be taken to Missouri and sold back to their owners for a significant financial gain. During the raid on the fort, Quantrill was sure to stay in the rear to ensure that Stewart did not see him.

It is conceivable Quantrill felt that by getting close to Jayhawkers in Lawrence, such as Stewart, he might be able to convince some of them to go on a raid into Missouri, where he would turn on them and hand them over to the Missouri authorities and thus earn the reward for their capture. It appears that Stewart never fully trusted Quantrill and would not agree to accompany him.

Was this double life of bushwhacker on the north side of the Kansas River and abolitionist on the south side of the river done purposefully? We must assume so, based on future events. There is no denying that having two different identities, on each side of the river, was certainly a risky venture, as it was not uncommon for people on both sides of the river to share acquaintances. It is possible that his bushwhacker friends at the ferry landing were in on the scheme, but that is a bit hard to fathom as it is unlikely that 20-year-old Quantrill, or Charley Hart, was any sort of a leader among these older, more grizzled men who loitered on the north side of the river. It is also hard to believe that Quantrill was the mastermind of this undercover plan which would necessarily include the complicity of these older men.

Quantrill, near the end of his time in Lawrence, would begin to wear out his welcome in the anti-slavery town. Douglas County Attorney, Samuel A Riggs indicted Quantrill (still going by Charley Hart) for arson, kidnapping, burglary and larceny for actions taken around the Lawrence area. Until the start of the war, Quantrill would be watching over his shoulder and avoiding law enforcement for these crimes.

It was during his time in Lawrence that "Charley Hart" began telling the story of his older brother's murder by bloodthirsty Kansans to any pro-slavery men that would listen. The story was that he and his older brother were camped outside Lawrence when they were attacked by free-state Kansans. The Kansans killed his brother and left him for dead. He would survive this attack and be nursed back to health by an Indian woman. He would then tell how he tracked down his attackers and eventually get his revenge by killing them all. As mentioned earlier in this chapter, the problem with this story is that Quantrill had no older brother, he was the oldest child in his family. That said, the story was a crowd-pleaser and he would tell it repeatedly in some of the finest houses in Missouri (Schultz 2).

There is an alternate version of this story that is told by William Gregg and John Edwards, both contemporaries and fans of Quantrill. Their account contends that Quantrill never said that his companion was his brother and that fact was something that had been misconstrued by a listener, who then passed it on with that detail as the heart of the story. In this version of the story, the character of Charley Hart was an identity that Quantrill adopted so he could infiltrate the Jayhawker groups and search for the men that attacked him and his companion (Peterson 16). This is another scenario where the actions of Quantrill look very different depending on which source you are reading. In fairness, either

Figure 61: The Morgan Walker Farm was located at the current location of Pink Hill Park in Blue Springs, Missouri.

story could be true. Adequate sources do not exist, which can confirm or prove false, one version as compared to the other. The reader will

Figure 62: Morgan Walker

need to look at the entirety of the information and decide which story they choose to believe.

In December of 1860, Quantrill convinced four abolitionists in Lawrence to accompany him into Missouri, where he proposed to raid the farm of Morgan Walker, who was said to have an impressive spread of over a thousand acres. He also had more than 30 slaves, over 100 horses and mules and at least $5,000 in cash on the farm. The small group would spend several days casing out the farm and making plans for the raid. What Quantrill's team of Kansans didn't know is that he had already double-crossed them by going to Walker's sons and telling them about the upcoming raid in exchange for a place to stay for a few weeks. He was worried Kansans were going to come looking for him if news of his treachery reached them.

Quantrill led the raid as planned, but after being forewarned of the attack, the Walkers had enlisted some neighbors to help them defend their property. Quantrill broke into the house and yelled that they were there taking "his niggers, horses and money" at which point Walker's neighbors rose from their hiding places around the property and opened fire, killing one of the Kansans who was standing on the porch as a guard. At this point, gunfire erupted from both sides and the raiders, several of whom were wounded, would scramble back to their horses and ride away.

Walker would quickly organize a group of men to hunt down the two members of the raiding party who had escaped. The Walker posse would eventually track both remaining men down and kill them. Legend has it that Quantrill held a pistol to the head of one of the raiders, Chalkley Lipsey. He pulled the trigger to ensure that Lipsey did not get back to Kansas and tell others that Quantrill had betrayed them. Months later, Quantrill, by now a famous leader of his own guerilla band, would tell his men that he shot Lipsey at point-blank range because the Jayhawker was a member of the group of men who had murdered his brother years earlier on the Sante Fe Trail. The story of the murdered brother is a common theme for Quantrill. In his book, Edward E. Leslie surmises that Quantrill uses this story to gain some credibility from his men. Regarding Lipsey's death, Walker, who was present, consistently maintained that this story was untrue and that while Lipsey was killed, Quantrill had not pulled the trigger.

Figure 63: Image of Quantrill likely taken around 1861. Note that Quantrill is wearing a guerrilla shirt. Image courtesy of www.canteymyerscollection.com

True to his word, Walker allowed Quantrill to stay with his family at the farm for some time after the raid. In the next couple of days, the Jackson County Sheriff came out to the farm and asked Quantrill to make a statement. There were several of Walker's neighbors who felt that Quantrill should have been killed with the other Jayhawkers. To prevent this from happening, the Sheriff took Quantrill to the Jackson County jail where he was kept for his own safety. Walker went to the jail and convinced the Sheriff to release Quantrill into his custody and protection.

While in town, Walker bought Quantrill a new set of clothes and let others know that Quantrill was under his protection and if anyone wanted to hurt him, they would do it "over his dead body". Walker and Quantrill returned to the Walker farm where he stayed for a few more days. Walker, concerned that his family and farm were in danger due to Quantrill's presence, gave him fifty dollars and a horse and asked him to leave for a few weeks until things cooled off.

On January 29, 1861, Kansas would officially join the Union as a free-state, eliminating the ambiguity around who was on the right side of the slave or free-state issue, at least in the eyes of the government. Respecting Walker's wishes for him to leave, Quantrill spent February of 1861, roaming around the border region, spending time on both sides of the state line. During this time, he would spend a few nights in the Paola jail, but was quickly released due to the efforts of some attorney friends in Paola. Returning to Missouri, in early March, he took up residence back in Jackson County with his friend, Mark Gill, who, with his wife and six daughters, owned a farm bordering Morgan Walker's property.

The American Civil War began with the attack and ultimate surrender of Fort Sumter on April 13, 1861. Quantrill's new housemate, Mark Gill, would abandon his home near Blue Springs and take his slaves to Texas where he felt they would be safe from federal forces. Quantrill, with nothing else to do, accompanied him to Texas where he stayed with Gill for a while but soon went out looking for more action.

He found that action north of the Texas border in the Cherokee Indian Nation, now Oklahoma, where he met Joel Mayes. Mayes was a half Scottish, half Cherokee man who would later become the Chief of the Cherokee Nation. Mayes, a Confederate Sympathizer, formed a company of Cherokees who would fight for the Confederacy. It was while riding with Mayes' outfit that Quantrill learned many of the guerrilla tactics that would make him famous when leading his band of

Bushwhackers. Mayes placed his company under the command of General Sterling Price with whom they would fight in the Battle of Wilson's Creek outside of Springfield, Missouri, in August of 1861.

Figure 64: Chief Joel Bryan Mayes of the Cherokee Nation

After the Confederate victory at Wilson's Creek, Mayes would take his men and leave General Price to head south to resupply his ammunition. Quantrill would stay on with General Price and enlist as a private in the Confederate Army. During his time serving under General Price, he would gain battle experience at the battles of Dry Wood Creek and Lexington. After the Confederate victory at Lexington, Price and his army would head south to Neosho, Missouri. Meanwhile, Major General John C. Fremont, Union Commander of the West, was marching a large force of 38,000 Union troops from Jefferson City to drive Price and his army out of central Missouri.

Quantrill would leave Price's army during the retreat to Neosho, although he did not desert as some historians have maintained. Rather, General Price had told his men to take leave and go home. His army had been inundated with new recruits since his victories at Wilson's Creek and Lexington, which had created a significant shortage of supplies for his command. (Leslie, pg. 94) This

Figure 65: Confederate General Sterling Price

parole of many of his troops would allow Price to feed and train his new recruits. Price hoped that most of the paroled men would return to the command after a visit home.

Back in west-central Missouri in the fall of 1861 and living at the, now empty, Mark Gill farm near Blue Springs, Quantrill began riding with Andrew Walker, son of Morgan Walker. Andrew Walker had formed a "home guard" unit of men whose purpose was to "guard" the local area residents against Jayhawkers terrorizing the Missouri border counties. Shortly after he started riding with Walker's home guard unit, Quantrill and Walker received intelligence that a band of Jayhawkers were in the area. In response, the two men raised a group of about ten men and headed out to intercept the Kansans. Their chase led them to the farm of Strawder Stone, where they arrived to find the house had already been robbed and was still on fire. The woman of the house was bleeding from a head wound that had been given to her by one of the Jayhawkers who had struck her with a pistol. The striking of a woman was said to have enraged the Missourians and they left the Stone farm and headed to the Billy Thompson homestead, not far away. They arrived at the Thompson home to find the house burning and the Jayhawkers, having just finished their brutal work, mounting up to leave. The Missourians rode into the yard with their guns blazing, immediately killing the man who had struck Mrs. Stone and wounding several other Jayhawkers before the Kansans could make their escape. Two more of the Jayhawkers reportedly died later in Independence from their wounds.

Remember that Missouri was a Union state and the authorities, taking their lead from the Union leaders in Independence, decided that something had to be done about the men who had killed the Kansans who were likely acting as federal troops. The Jayhawkers were sent home and the authorities arrested Strawder Stone and Billy Thompson for the murder of three Jayhawkers who had died in the raid. Quantrill immediately went to Independence and swore that Strawder and Thompson had nothing to do with the shooting and took the blame for the killing of the three Jayhawkers. Strangely, the authorities decided not to arrest Quantrill even though he had confessed to these murders. This selfless act by Quantrill would make him a local hero in the Blue Springs area, at least among the Southern Sympathizers.

During the fall and winter of 1861, Quantrill spent his time riding with Walker's "home guard" unit to repel and chase multiple Jayhawk bands which were frequently raiding in the Blue Springs area. In late 1861, Morgan Walker, feared for his son Andrew's life because the Jayhawkers were now able to commit their atrocities as volunteer federal forces. He convinced his son to stop leading the home guard and to return home to help him on the farm. This left a leadership void among Walker's men. Twenty-four-year-old William Clarke Quantrill would be the man to fill that void.

Why did men follow Quantrill? The reasons are clear when one looks at his resume for the job at this point in his life.

- He was educated, well-liked and charismatic
- He was a masterful horseman and could match any man with a gun
- He had experience and had been trained in guerilla warfare tactics during his time riding with the Cherokee Nation
- He had served in the regular army, albeit briefly, and was knowledgeable of military discipline and tactics
- He was a local hero due to his actions that freed Strawder Stone and Billy Thompson

The men's choice for a leader would turn out to be a good one. Whether you approve of his ideas and methods or not, there is little argument that Quantrill was a very effective leader during his short time in the national spotlight (Leslie 96).

During the winter of 1861-1862, Quantrill and his men were still acting as more state guards than Bushwhackers. Early on under Quantrill's leadership, his command stayed in Missouri. Quantrill and his men protected local Southern Sympathizers by doing everything they could to slow down or disrupt the actions of the jayhawking forces that were continually raiding Missouri farms and communities. These activities often included disrupting federal supply chains by attacking shipments and stealing or destroying goods in those shipments meant for the Union forces in the area. Of course, Quantrill and his raiders are best known for their Raid of Lawrence in 1863. This and other raids into Kansas, including Olathe, were carried out in late 1862 and early

1863 in response to Lane and Jennison's raids into Missouri during the winter of 1861-8162. Another example of revenge driving strategy.

In the early days of Quantrill's command, he led only about 15 men, most of whom were Jackson County residents. A few notable names in that original group of fifteen include: Perry Hoy, William H Gregg and George Todd. They would later be joined by even more notable figures

Figure 66: Captain William Gregg (left) and George Todd

such as; Frank and Jesse James, Cole and Bob Younger and William (Bloody Bill) Anderson.

While acting as a home guard unit, Quantrill and his men would act as sort of the Confederate version of law enforcement. In this role, Quantrill is said to have hunted down a Confederate deserter named George Searcy, who upon his capture by Quantrill and his men, was found to have at least 75 horses, deeds, mortgages and notes that belonged to others. Quantrill gave Searcy a quick trial and sentenced him to be hanged, which he was. After this, Quantrill returned the property that Searcy had stolen to the rightful owners. He did this, even though Searcy had largely stolen from pro-Union families. This act gave Quantrill and his band a bit of a "Robin Hood" type reputation in the area and fostered a more tolerant reputation, even among Union sympathizers.

Quantrill and his men were trying to do what they could to aid Missouri residents who were constantly being attacked and robbed by Kansas Jayhawkers, like Jim Lane, Charles "Doc" Jennison and Daniel Anthony, who in the winter of 1861 were acting "legally" under the guise of being sanctioned by the Union Army. These men and the troops they led, were punishing all Missourians, not just Southern Sympathizers. The list below shows military actions by each side from July 1861 through January 1862. This should give the reader an idea of why a Missouri resident might desire to join or support one of these "Home Guard" units.

Date	Event	Leader(s)	Aggressor
June 19, 1861	Independence	Jennison	Jayhawkers
July 20, 1861	Morristown, MO	Jennison	Jayhawkers
July 26, 1861	Harrisonville, MO	Jennison	Jayhawkers
Sept 17, 1861	Morristown, MO	Montgomery	Jayhawkers
Sept 19, 1861	Papinville, MO	Lane	Jayhawkers
Sept 26, 1861	Osceola, MO	Lane	Jayhawkers
Oct 14, 1861	Humboldt, KS	Livingston	CSA
Oct 16, 1861	Pleasant Hill, MO	Lane	Jayhawkers
Oct 17, 1861	Kingsville, MO	Lane	Jayhawkers
Oct 18, 1861	Rose Hill, MO	Lane	Jayhawkers
Oct 20, 1861	Clinton, MO	Lane	Jayhawkers
Oct 21, 1861	Humansville, MO	Lane	Jayhawkers
Oct 1861	Pleasant Hill, MO	Lane	Jayhawkers
Oct 22, 1861	Gardner, KS	Yeager	Bushwhackers
Nov 14, 1861	Independence, MO	Jennison/Anthony	Jayhawkers
Nov 22, 1861	Pleasant Hill, MO	Jennison/Anthony	Jayhawkers
Nov 1861	West Point, MO	Jennison/Anthony	Jayhawkers
Dec 1861	Morristown, MO	Jennison Anthony	Jayhawkers
Dec 11, 1861	Potosi, KS	Clement	Bushwhackers
Dec 12, 1861	Papinville, MO	Stewart	Jayhawkers
Dec 12, 1861	Butler, MO	Stewart	Jayhawkers
Jan 1, 1862	Dayton, MO	Jennison/Anthony	Jayhawkers
Jan 9, 1862	Columbus, MO	Jennison/Anthony	Jayhawkers
Feb 21, 1862	Independence	Quantrill	Bushwhackers
Mar 7, 1862	Aubry, KS	Quantrill	Bushwhackers
July 11, 1862	Battle of the Ravines, Pleasant Hill, MO	Quantrill	Equal pitched battle
Aug 11, 1862	Independence, MO (Attack on Federal Garrison)	Quantrill	Bushwhackers + CSA
Sept 7, 1862	Olathe, KS	Quantrill	Bushwhackers
Oct 17, 1862	Shawnee, KS	Quantrill	Bushwhackers

Figure 67: List of Border War Raids between June '61 - September '62. Blue lines are Union/Jayhawker raids, Butternut are Bushwhacker raids

The previous chart shows the major events that took place on the border from July 1861 through the Olathe Raid in September 1862. The chart does not include battles between regular Union and Confederate forces, it also does not include instances where individual homesteads were destroyed. The Bushwhackers were not idle during the winter of 1861-1862, but as previously mentioned much of their activity was centered around harassing federal forces, such as Jim Lane and Doc Jennison's troops that were terrorizing Missouri at this time.

The number of Missouri homes burned to the ground by Jayhawkers during 1861 and 1862 total more than 2,400. A detailed list of the Missouri homes burned can be found at http://quantrillsguerrillas.com in an article entitled, "Approximate number of Missouri homes burned by jayhawkers-Redleg's". (Peterson, burned). Conversely, the Bushwhacker groups were not known for the burning of towns and homes. It did happen, but not on a regular basis. This is likely because the Bushwhackers were operating in their backyard as opposed to the Jayhawkers who were in "enemy" territory. The Jayhawkers were trying to inflict as much destruction as possible. For Quantrill specifically, he and his men did not burn the Kansas towns that they raided. This was true until the famous Raid of Lawrence in 1863, where approximately 100 buildings were burned. Before Lawrence, Quantrill's men looted and inflicted significant damage to the buildings in towns they raided, but rarely did they burn them to the ground.

Quantrill's first known raid into Kansas occurred at daybreak on March 7th, 1862, when he and forty of his men rode into Aubry, now a part of present-day Stillwell. The band entered town yelling loudly and shooting pistols in the air. On their way past a local inn, Quantrill looked up and saw two men looking down from an upstairs window. He took aim and shot one of them in the forehead. A shot he would later call "a damn good shot". He learned later that the man he had shot was Abraham Ellis, who happened to be the Stanton Superintendent of Schools.

Ellis, who had hired Quantrill to teach in that district in 1859, staggered into the downstairs of the inn where Quantrill was sitting after the town was under control. Upon seeing Ellis, Quantrill quickly grabbed a rag and started wiping the blood away from the wound. "Ellis, I am damned sorry I shot you – you are one of the Kansas men I do not want to shoot," said Quantrill. Ellis, even though he was shot in the head, would survive and bear the scar on his forehead for the rest of his life. The ball and bone fragments from this injury are currently in the Army and Navy Medical Museum in Washington, D.C.

Figure 68: Aubry, Kansas, is now a part of Stillwell, Kansas. On the right is an image of Abraham "Bullethole" Ellis, Image courtesy of Kansas State Historical Society

During their raid of Aubry, Quantrill's raiders killed five men, robbed every man in town and burned down one local building. They rode out of town back to Missouri easily eluding the union pursuit (Castel 71). Quantrill made sure that Abraham Ellis got his money and his horse back before the raiders left town.

Leslie points out that even though Quantrill may have been involved in some less than legal activities prior to 1861, once the war began, Quantrill seemed to consider himself, and his men, soldiers, who were thus bound by military rules of conduct. By all accounts, he made sure that women were treated properly, kept his promises to enemy commanders, granted paroles to prisoners and tried to exchange prisoners, all of which were proper military protocol at the time.

Quantrill's treatment of prisoners changed when, facing the difficulty in catching the likes of Quantrill and other Bushwhacker groups, General Henry W. Halleck, commander of the Department of Missouri, would issue General Order Number 2 on March 13, 1861. Order number 2 was a proclamation that "outlawed" guerrillas and decreed that, "they will not, if captured, be treated as ordinary prisoners of war, but will be hung as robbers and murderers." At the time this order was issued, Quantrill was not well-known, and the order was likely issued in response to other guerrilla bands operating around the state (Schultz 85). The order would impact all guerrilla units. It is this order and the subsequent behavior of the Union troops in Missouri, that led Quantrill to alter his treatment of enemy prisoners going forward. It would be incorrect to say that Quantrill executed all prisoners because there are several instances, such as Olathe, where that is simply not true. However, it would be fair to say that Quantrill's "gentlemanly" treatment of prisoners changed drastically after the Halleck proclamation.

Quantrill did not hear about Halleck's edict until approximately five days after it was issued. At this time, he reportedly read the proclamation to his men and gave them an opportunity to leave the unit due to the increased danger that being part of a guerrilla group brought with it. Of the sixty men with him at the time, forty-five opted to stay and fifteen returned to their farms. Most of the fifteen would return to the unit within the month as the actions of the Jayhawkers made it very difficult to live normal lives on their farms. These men likely felt that the only option they had was to go back to the bushwhacking groups. After reading Order

Figure 69: Major General Henry W. Halleck, Commander of the Department of Missouri

Number 2 in a local paper, Quantrill sent a note to Halleck saying, "For every man of mine you kill, I will kill ten of yours" (Peterson, 111).

A previously mentioned, by January of 1862, Quantrill and his men had expanded their activities from simply protecting the area against Jayhawkers to include harassing and attacking federal troops. These hit and run raids were carefully planned and commonly used the element of surprise. On February 3, 1862, a Union captain sent this letter to Brigadier General John Pope:

General, I have just returned from an expedition which I was compelled to undertake in search of the notorious Quantrell [sic] and his gang of robbers in the vicinity of Blue Springs. . . . I have seen this infamous scoundrel rob mails, steal coaches and horses, and commit other similar outrages upon society even within sight of this city [Independence]. Mounted on the best horses of the country, he has defied pursuit, making his camp in the bottoms of the Little Blue River, roving over a circuit of 30 miles. (Leslie 104)

However, Quantrill's unit was not limited to only harassment of federal troops. He and his men would also target any Union families still left in the area, the number of which was dwindling. Using many of the same tactics used by Jayhawker units against Southern Sympathizers, his men would make life for Unionists remaining in the rural areas of western Missouri very unpleasant. He is said to have announced to anyone supporting the Union in the area, "Don't bother planting crops, as you won't be around to see them harvested."

Capturing Quantrill and his men was made more difficult by the fact that southern sympathizing people in rural Missouri would aid, feed and supply the guerillas keeping their men and their horses fit and strong so they could evade authorities. Bettie Muri, a small child at the time, remembers Union soldiers eating at their house, even though her father was an officer in the Confederate Army. Muri remembers her mother feeding Union soldiers during the day and Bushwhackers at night (Schwenk 89).

One of the tactics that Quantrill used to frustrate the pursuit of his men was to quickly disband his command after a skirmish. He would tell his men to go home, thus scattering them in all directions, making them nearly impossible to follow or track, since the one trail would turn into multiple trails. The guerrillas' familiarity with the land and its many ravines and creeks made them particularly difficult to track. In addition, they generally had no set "camp" which meant that there was no target for Union soldiers to attack. Of course, once the guerrillas arrived at home, there were many family members and neighbors who were willing to attest that they had been home all the time and could not have possibly taken part in any sort of raid.

One Quantrill attack is summed up by historian Duane Schultz:

When the soldiers drew close the bushwhackers would suddenly come charging out of the brush on horseback screaming the terrifying rebel yell and blazing away with their pistols. In a matter of seconds, the whole affair would be over. The guerrillas would strip their victims' bodies, round up their horses, and disappear once more into the forests and thickets. (80)

On April 21, 1862, the Congress of the Confederate States of America attempted to counter the order by General Halleck by passing the "Partisan Ranger Act of 1862". This act was an attempt to legitimatize the men riding with the Bushwhacker units by calling them Confederate Soldiers and thus giving them the protections that would have been afforded soldiers in times of war. This attempt by the Confederacy to help the bushwhacking groups was largely ignored by the Union authorities. The practice of "no quarter" was continued by all Union forces operating in Missouri when it came to their treatment of captured guerilla fighters.

The spring of 1862 was a busy time for Quantrill and the Union army who were doing everything in their power to bring the Bushwhacker raids under control in the region. During this time, on three different occasions, Quantrill and smaller groups of his men were surrounded in homes that they were using for hideouts. In each instance, the Union soldiers are said to have had the guerrillas surrounded but were unable to stop the Bushwhackers from escaping. At some point during the skirmish, the guerrillas would make a break for it and run for the woods. Once into the woods, the men would scatter. While each of these instances usually resulted in a few Bushwhacker casualties, wounded men and the loss of horses, they never resulted in mass captures nor the capture of Quantrill himself. These continued failures to capture Quantrill would frustrate Union authorities and lead to the more brutal treatment of locals by the Union forces trying to bring the Bushwhackers to justice.

In late July 1862, recruiting for the Confederacy and the Partisan Ranger units roaming Missouri was given a shot in the arm by Union Brigadier General John M. Schofield, when he issued Order Number 19. Order Number 19 stated that all able-bodied male Missourians were required to enlist in the state militia "for the purpose of exterminating the guerrillas that infest our state." He also restated Halleck's order in March by calling all the Missourians riding in the partisan units "robbers and assassins" and ordering that, if captured, they should be immediately "shot down on the spot".

This order put every man in Missouri in a tough position, regardless of their political affiliation. By joining the state militia, and thus following Schofield's orders, they would likely be asked to hunt down and possibly kill family members, friends and neighbors who had chosen to ride with one of the guerrilla bands. Many of the men who were not already serving in one of the two armies, had been, thus far, able to walk the line between the two sides of the conflict. With Order Number 19, they were forced to publicly choose a side. Many of these men chose to enlist in the Confederate Army or to join one of the guerrilla bands such as the one led by William Quantrill. With the help of this order, Quantrill's band, in early August grew to over three hundred men. Even though his command numbered over 300, it is important to note that this did not mean that there was a large camp of these men. The guerrilla model continued to operate in small individual groups with only very loose coordination. If larger numbers were needed for a certain mission, the call would go out and the smaller units would come together.

In early August, recovering from a bullet to the thigh from a run-in with Union troops, Quantrill teamed up with regular Confederate troops to attack the federal garrison in the city of Independence. While he was recuperating from his injury, Quantrill directed the scouting of the operation and helped to plan the attack. Quantrill's men would hold the actual town while the Confederate troops, led by Colonel John T. Hughes, would attack the Union soldiers who were camped a half-mile from the town square. Except for Colonel Hughes being killed, the plan went off without a hitch. After fierce fighting, the Federal Commander, Lieutenant Colonel James T. Buel surrendered the town, his men, and all their supplies to the acting Confederate commander, Colonel Gideon W. Thompson. Buel's one condition for the surrender of his men was that none of them would be given to Quantrill fearing they would be executed if they were turned over to the guerrilla leader. While Quantrill did not get any of the 150 men that were taken prisoner, he and his men did enjoy a large share of the captured horses, ammunition and supplies that were taken after the battle. Many Southern Sympathizers gave Quantrill's guerrillas credit for the taking of Independence since it was his men who did most of the fighting in the town itself.

Figure 70: Quantrill, flanked by two of his men, Oliver (right) and George Shepherd (left)

After the fighting at Independence, Colonel Thompson officially mustered Quantrill and 120 of his men into the "Southern Service" as Partisan Rangers. Quantrill was named Captain, with William Haller, George Todd and William Gregg named first, second and third Lieutenants respectively (Castel 92). This official act was largely cere-monial as Quantrill and his men already consid-ered themselves Partisan Rangers. It did give Quantrill something he had always wanted, a sense of legitimacy. It would also cause him problems when one of his men, an orderly, was killed in a skirmish. Upon searching the body of the dead guerrilla, federal soldiers found a list of men who had been mustered into the Confederate Army under The Partisan Ranger Act. The names on this list surprised federal authorities as many of them were men whom they had no idea had been riding with a guerrilla unit. The list became a death sentence for anyone whose name appeared on it.

By late August 1862, due to the success of his operations and the recruiting boost provided to the Missouri Partisans due to Order Number 19, Quantrill's command was large in numbers and fully supplied. The stage was now set for the raid on Olathe.

Olathe, 1862

Note to Reader: The information in this next chapter is the result of extensive research into the makeup of the Olathe downtown in 1862 at the time of Quantrill's raid. Because there are no existing maps from this time frame, my research focused on later maps (1874 is the earliest known plat map in existence), land records, newspaper advertisements and most importantly eyewitness accounts from this time. The maps in this section are based on that research and the creation of these maps is based on the compilation of all the different sources as to where things might have been located at the time. This is an inexact science and some of the locations on the map are best guesses based on the records available.

The Olathe Town Company was founded in 1857 under a charter granted by the "Bogus Legislature". The first group of trustees was installed in 1859 and included Jonathan Millikin, J.T. Barton, S. F. Hill, A.J. Clemmans and L.S. Cornwall. Other prominent citizens at that time could purchase shares of the company and would later use those shares to purchase other properties throughout the town.

In early September of 1862, the city of Olathe, population 520, would have been a busy, but peaceful place. There would be traffic on the dirt streets because Olathe was the county seat of Johnson County. Legal matters would bring visitors to town to conduct business with the many lawyers that had offices in the city. Visitors would also see a large amount of military activity, particularly after the Civil War started in 1861, as the town was home to a recruiting station for the Union Army. The recruiting station was commanded by J.E. Hayes. The downtown was centered around a large open block, commonly referred to as the "public square". The first courthouse, not officially purchased by the county until 1862, was not in the public square. Rather, it was across the street on the southwest corner of the square. A "3 board fence" surrounded the public square. It was common around this time that public squares would be fenced, and that space was used for public gatherings or military drills. The streets around the square would be full of foot, horse and wagon traffic all of which would have created significant dust in dry weather and a muddy mess in wet weather.

While my research did not extend to the areas that were more than one block off the public square, it is important to have some idea of what the Olathe countryside would have looked like in 1862. The original town was laid out by the Olathe Town Company to extend several blocks away from the public square. Official roads and blocks would not have existed and most of the roads more than one block off the square would likely have been dirt trails and would not have been laid out in a nice grid-like later maps depict. One eyewitness talks about

Figure 71: These images show what the buildings around the Olathe square would have looked like in 1862. (left) Fort Smith, Arkansas, (center) Olathe, Kansas 1884, (right) Dodge City, Kansas

the old trail that ran roughly where you see it on the following map. It is likely that travelers coming down Sante Fe Street from points north and east would have used this trail rather than Sante Fe Street if they were headed to the south side of the square. Most of the area around the downtown was sparsely populated with farms dotting the landscape. The map is meant to provide an idea of what the town and surrounding area may have looked like at this time in history. The locations of homes more than a block off the square are not historically accurate but have been added to give the reader an idea of what the surrounding countryside might have looked like in 1862.

Determining the ownership of city lots and buildings in Olathe during this period is tricky. The Olathe Town Company owned all the lots originally and most of the early land transactions in the Olathe ledgers are of those founders speculating on certain lots by purchasing multiple lots either using cash or shares that they owned in the town company. This speculation would continue over the next twenty years in Olathe. The ledger books are full of transactions for certain men who did a great deal of the speculation. A review of the land transactions from 1857 – 1870 shows that these speculators would buy, sell and trade land frequently. Sometimes the sale price would be a few thousand dollars and sometimes it would be one dollar. Why the difference? Was something else included with the land? Did they just trade parcels? Did they lose it in a poker game? Unfortunately, the records don't provide that detail.

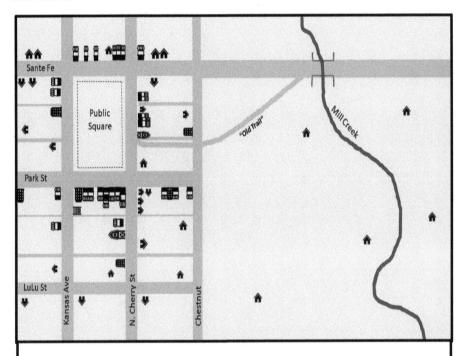

Figure 72: 1862 Map of Olathe downtown. Icons show dwellings, shops/offices, hotels, livery barns or tradesman shops

It was also common that, on many city lots, the owner of the land and building might not be the person who occupied that space with his home or shop. My research has uncovered many newspaper advertisements that show that a certain person had a store on a certain side of the square, but there is no corresponding land transaction for that person for that side of the square. Of course, spoiler alert, many of the town records were destroyed during Quantrill's raid on Olathe.

Most of the buildings on the square at this time would have been one or two-story buildings made of wood, brick or stone. The upstairs of the 2-story buildings often served as homes or apartments for single men, or as lodging for soldiers or travelers passing through town. Olathe had at least three saloons around the square. The 1884 Sanborn Insurance Company Map, published over 20 years later, shows as many as five billiard halls in the four blocks surrounding the public square. The blocks on the east and south of the square would have been the most densely populated, but there still would have been open lots in those blocks. Some of the buildings would have shared common walls, but many would not and were built as standalone structures.

East Side

The businesses across Cherry street, east of the public square would have likely included, several homes, the Star Saloon, Attorney AJ Hill's offices, a drugstore, a livery stable, and a stone post office building.

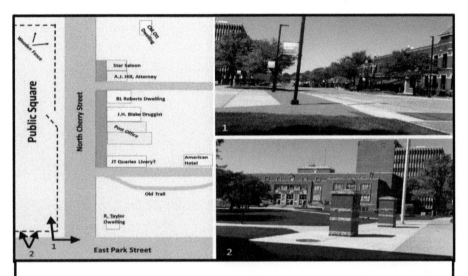

Figure 73: 1862 map (left) and 2020 map (right) of the east side of the square. Blue = Stone, Yellow = Wood. Numbers show the placement of the camera for the 2020 images

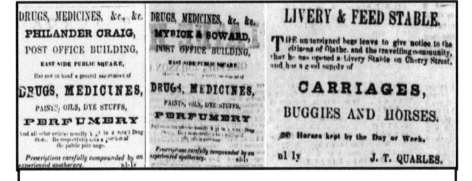

Figure 74: Advertisements for eastside businesses from the Olathe Herald, August 9, 1860. The two druggists were in the Post Office Building. I believe that Quarles Livery was located just south of the Post Office Building

South Side

To the south, across Park Street, you would see the Courthouse, Hoff's Grocery and Provision Store, Sutton's Dry Goods Store, the offices of Lecompton and Burris Attorneys at Law and J.E. Hayes Storeroom. "Colonel" J.E. Hayes was a local builder and landowner who built many of the buildings around town. The empty space on this block may have been filled by another tavern. Research tells us that

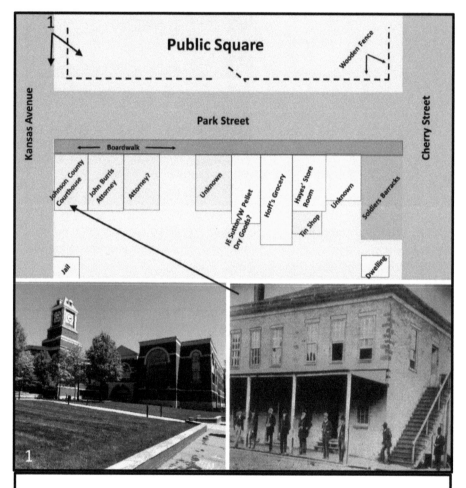

Figure 75: Map of Park Street on the south side of the Public square. This section of Park Street was removed when the Johnson County Administration Building (bottom left) was erected in 1992. (bottom right) First Johnson County Courthouse, purchased by the County in 1862 for $900

there were three on the square, but I have only found records for two of them. Directly behind the courthouse, but not attached, was the county calaboose. Calaboose was the name for the "jail" during this time frame.

This section of Park Street no longer exists. The street was removed in the early 1990s when the Johnson County Administration building was built directly on top of where this section of Park Street would have been located. The street would have run directly between what is today East Park Street and West Park Street.

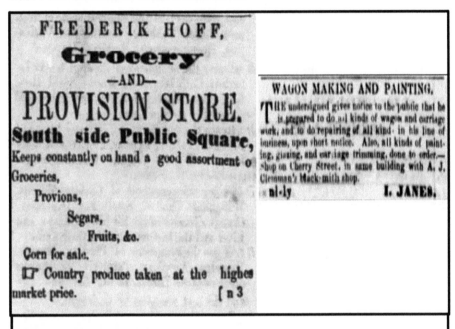

Figure 76: On the right is an advertisement for Hoff Grocery and Provision Store which appeared in the May 30, 1861, edition of the Olathe Mirror. On the left is an advertisement for Wagon Making and Painting from the August 9, 1861, Olathe Herald. This business would have been on Cherry Street a block south of the square facing east.

West Side

The west side of the square, across Kansas Avenue, was less densely populated than the eastern and southern sides. This block would have been dominated by the Turpin House, which would later become the Avenue Hotel. The Turpin House was a hotel and restaurant owned by A. J. Turpin, a known Southern Sympathizer whose son rode with Quantrill. Quantrill was said to have visited the house for dinner in April of 1861. The Turpin House, located where the current jail is today, would have been a two-story structure that stretched over two "city lots" with a stable just off the southwest corner of the building.

To the north of the Turpin House, there would have been two small buildings, possibly a shop and an attorney's office. In the middle of the block was S.F Hill's store. Hill, one of the town's leading carpenters,

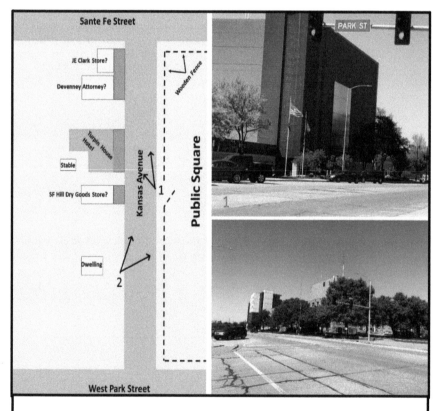

Figure 77: Map shows Kansas Avenue west of the public square in 1862. Images on the right show the same block in 2020

would be the man who was hired by the town to build the fence around the public square in 1860. Hill and his wife lived in a home just a few lots south of their store. At some point, there would be a large lumberyard at the southern end of this block, but I was unable to find any land transactions to prove that this existed in 1862.

Figure 78: Turpin House and S.F. Hill advertisements from the August 9, 1860, Olathe Herald. Dr. J.P. Hill advertisement from the May 30, 1861 Olathe Mirror.

North Side

The north side of the public square would have been home to a hardware store, a few homes, a bakery, a drug store and another saloon. J.M. Giffin, an attorney, owned a house and another building on this block, from which he published and was editor of the Olathe Herald, a Southern Sympathizing newspaper.   The Olathe Hotel would eventually be opened in 1903 on the northwest corner of Sante Fe and Cherry Street, but in 1862 this corner would have housed a new single-story stone building erected by Mr. Tillotson where he ran a hardware store.

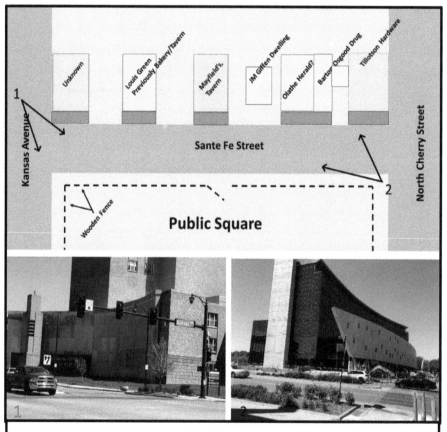

Figure 79: Map of the block on the north side of the public square in 1862. Bottom left is the 1952 Courthouse located on the public square. In the right is the 2020 Courthouse directly across Sante Fe Street to the north from the 1952 Courthouse.

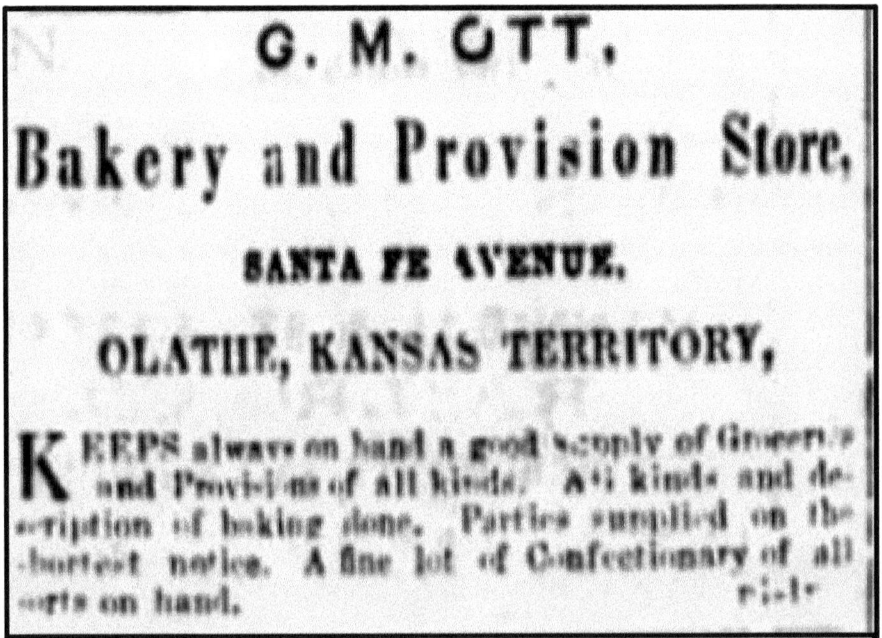

G. M. OTT,

Bakery and Provision Store,

SANTA FE AVENUE,

OLATHE, KANSAS TERRITORY,

KEEPS always on hand a good supply of Groceries and Provisions of all kinds. All kinds and description of baking done. Parties supplied on the shortest notice. A fine lot of Confectionary of all sorts on hand.

Figure 80: Advertisement printed on August 9, 1860, in the Olathe Herald for C.M. Ott's Bakery. Ott would own many properties around the square in the next several years. Ott is the Great-Great Grandfather of the author.

Park Street (East of Public Square)

In 1862, East Park Street would have only contained a few buildings. The two eastern corners of the intersection with Cherry Street, would have been occupied by multiple houses. Two of these houses were owned by Judge J.P. Campbell, a known Southern Sympathizer on the southeast corner and the other by Richard Taylor, son of U.S. President Zachary Taylor, on the northeast corner. On the south side of Park Street, heading east, there would have been at least one more house, as well as a two-story building that served a dual purpose as the Presbyterian Church and barracks for soldiers. At the end of the southern side of East Park, there would have been a hardware store and a home directly behind the store to the south.

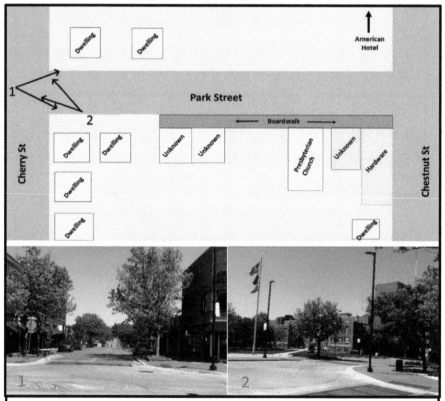

Figure 81: Map shows 1862 East Park Street which was directly south and east of the public square. Image 1 shows the 2020 view down East Park Street to the east. Image 2 shows a view of the public square, now occupied by the 1952 Courthouse to the northeast.

Based on land records from this time, the north side of Park Street, between Cherry and Chestnut, would have been largely vacant except for the houses on the eastern corner. This may be because the "old trail" ran through this block and building something in that block would have put those buildings directly across the old trail. Eventually, this block would be full of businesses, but not in 1862. We do know that the American Hotel, built and owned by J.E. Hayes, was built about 100 yards to the north of Park Street, facing Chestnut Street. One account describes the American Hotel as a fine hotel that was used to house soldiers during the war. This tells us that before the war, the American Hotel was the "free-state" hotel while the Turpin House on Kansas Avenue was the "pro-slavery" hotel.

Make no mistake, even though Olathe was a bustling town in 1862, its citizens were also on edge. All of them, regardless of their political beliefs, were terrified that they would be the next border town attacked. Before and during the Civil War, the Union Army in Kansas seemed powerless in protecting the Kansas citizens from pro-slavery forces and later from Missouri Bushwhackers. John Francis, the editor of the *Olathe Mirror*, was very critical of the Commander of the Department of Kansas after raids in the nearby towns of Gardner and Aubry. Francis criticized the army for only sending troops after the towns had already been ransacked. He would prove prophetic when he wrote:

[Olathe] would receive protection here after Quantrill pays us a visit and kills about 20 men, then this "Bully Commander" . . . will send us a body of men for our protection" (Olathe Mirror, March 20, 1862).

Francis was correct in his perception that the ability of the Federal Army to protect Kansas towns was basically non-existent; however, towns like Olathe, never took protection of their lives and possessions into their own hands by establishing home guards and watch patrols. As you will see in the coming pages, Quantrill and his men rode into the Olathe Square on the night of September 6th, 1862, uncontested and without a peep of warning from any Olathe residents.

The Raid on Olathe

Note to Reader: The information in the next two chapters is pulled from a variety of sources such as published works, eyewitness accounts and newspaper articles written during and after the actual events. There are many discrepancies in these accounts as to certain details of the events between August 28th and October 14th. I have tried to access original accounts and reports where possible, but discrepancies still exist. I have used the facts that seem to be the most common and to make the most sense from a historic perspective. When there are significant differences, I have tried to let the reader know where the discrepancies exist and possible explanations.

"Perry Hoy is Executed!" These words, printed in the *St Louis Republican,* were the trigger that caused the raid on the city of Olathe. Perry Hoy was one of the original members of Quantrill's band of Bushwhackers and was taken prisoner by federal soldiers in the summer of 1982. Hoy was charged with the murders of a federal cavalry officer and the toll keeper of a bridge on the Little Blue River, southeast of Kansas City. Quantrill was trying to work out a prisoner exchange in which he would trade Lieutenant Levi Copeland, who was taken prisoner at the Battle of Lone Jack, for Perry Hoy. Lieutenant Copeland was being held prisoner by General Blunt, a Confederate General who was in the Kansas City area after the battle of Lone Jack and was preparing his men to move to Arkansas.

Perry Hoy was executed by federal authorities at Fort Leavenworth on July 28th, 1862. It took almost a month before news of the execution traveled to Quantrill and his band, who were camped on the Little Blue River, about three miles east of Lee's Summit. It was here that two of his men brought Quantrill a copy of *The St. Louis Republican*, which contained the news about Perry Hoy's execution. In his memoir, William Gregg writes:

Suddenly I saw a change in Quantrill's countenance, and the paper fell from his hand. Without saying a word, he drew a blank book from his pocket, penned a note on a leaf and folded and handed it to me, saying 'give this to [General] Blunt.

The note simply says, "Take Lieutenant Copeland out and shoot him, go to Woodsmall's camp, get two prisoners and shoot them" (Beilein 57).

Quantrill and his men remained at their camp for a few more days, awaiting word that the executions had been carried out. On September 4th, Quantrill ordered his men to get ready to ride. When Gregg asked Quantrill where they were going, Quantrill replied, "We

Figure 82: Solomon Perry Hoy, taken in March 1862. Perry Hoy was executed by a firing squad at Fort Leavenworth, Kansas, on July 28, 1862. Image courtesy of www.cantemyerscollection.com .

are going to Kansas and kill ten more men for poor Perry!" (Castel 96). The guerrillas left camp that day and spent the next night near Red Bridge, which was a small community south of Kansas City, just west of the Blue River. It was important for the Bushwhackers to get a good night's sleep. The next day would prove to be a very long one.

By midafternoon on September 6, 1862, the Bushwhackers were on the trail and headed for Olathe. Quantrill planned to raid the town after dark when most of the citizens were comfortably asleep in their beds. Sources vary on the number of men that Quantrill had with him. Some reports contend that there were as many as 250 men, while other accounts report as few as 60. The most commonly cited number is that he had approximately 140 raiders with him as he rode into Olathe. Olathe might have been seen as an easy target as it was only about ten

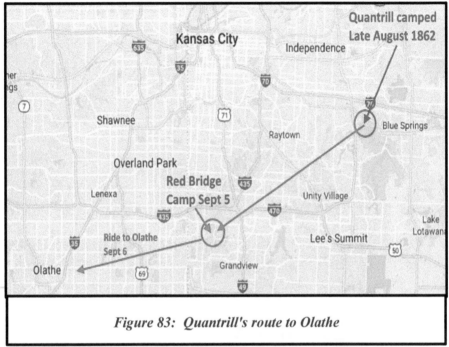

Figure 83: Quantrill's route to Olathe

miles from the border and was known to be sparsely defended.

The people of Olathe were also known for their staunch abolitionist stance, which only made the town a more attractive target for Quantrill and his men. Quantrill had likely been informed of the lack of readiness of the town's defenses by citizens who were currently living in the city. We know that one of Quantrill's men, Cliff Turpin, had been a resident of Olathe and his family still resided there, running the Turpin House Hotel. Cliff's mother had traveled to Missouri the previous day and returned the night of the raid. It is possible, but unconfirmed, that Turpin's mother provided intelligence as to the defenses of the town. The timing of her trip is certainly suspect (Kamberg).

The town leaders and the Federal Government had done a poor job of preparing Olathe for any type of attack. This lack of preparedness doesn't make Olathe different than most other Kansas towns, but one might have thought that Olathe's proximity to the border would have made them a little more vigilant about preparing for a possible attack. Olathe city leaders had probably been lulled into a false sense of security as there had not been a significant raid by Bushwhackers in

Kansas since the March raid of Aubry. It is likely that as time passed with no raids, the feeling of a need for proactive measures declined. There were likely discussions in the local taverns regarding possible Bushwhacker attacks and what measures should be taken to strengthen the town's defenses. Unfortunately, town leaders did not follow through on any of these thoughts, and on the evening of Saturday, September 6th, Quantrill and his Bushwhackers were able to ride into town without any resistance, nor warning from the citizens of Olathe.

Quantrill and his men crossed the border around nightfall and proceeded up Coffee Creek, where a small group of men split off and stopped at the residence of David Williams, about six miles east of Olathe in the Oxford Township. David William's son-in-law was a man named Frank Cook. Mr. Cook had just enlisted in the Union Army. His unit, the newly formed Twelfth Kansas Rifles, was based in Olathe and prepared to leave the area on Monday morning. Cook was visiting his wife at his in-laws to say goodbye before reporting for duty.

Mr. Cook had gone to bed for the evening and was in the back bedroom but upon hearing a commotion, he came to the front of the house to investigate. The ruckus was being caused by at least a dozen Bushwhackers who had entered the home uninvited. The raiders immediately took Cook prisoner as his wife, Sarah, begged for her husband's life. Mrs. Cook had a firm grip on her husband's arm and would not let go until one of the intruders told her that if she did not let go, he would "blow her damn brains out" (Hermon 2). She let go and they took him away. His body was found the next day in

Figure 84: Williams Family Cemetery. The burial place of Frank Cook is located at 148th Street and Quivira Road. The small cemetery is in a neighborhood between two backyards along Quivira Road.

a ravine on the northwest side of Olathe. He had been shot three times and his head had been bashed in with a cannonball. Later, one of the men who shot Frank Cook is said to have bragged about his execution and laughed at Mr. Cook's agony at the thought of "never seeing his little family again." The Bushwhacker also ridiculed Mr. Cook's prayers and petitions for mercy (Thavis). Frank Cook is buried in the Williams Family Cemetery at 148th Street and Quivira Road.

Continuing toward Olathe, the Bushwhackers next stopped at the home of John Judy approximately a mile and half east of the city. John Judy and his brother James had also just enlisted in the Union Army. Like Frank Cook, the Judy brothers were at home enjoying one last night with family before leaving to be full-time soldiers. The Judy house was probably chosen because the brothers' father, Reason Judy, was known to have recently fought for the Union in the Battle of Lone Jack. It was common for raiders on both sides of the border to use organized raids as excuses to settle old scores with someone they had known in the past. Some of Quantrill's men likely had a score to settle with Reason Judy.

Both Judy brothers were in bed when twelve to fifteen Bushwhackers entered the house and ordered the brothers to get dressed. While the brothers were getting dressed, the Bushwhackers ransacked the house, opening trunks, stealing valuables and smashing what they didn't want. During their time in the house, the Bush-whackers were said to have made inappropriate remarks to John's wife, while she cried and begged them to leave the men alone. At one point, one of the Bushwhackers told Mrs. Judy, "If you have much Union about you, you better work it off by crying, and we give you some cause enough" (Thavis).

Figure 85: John and James Judy Grave Site, Olathe Cemetery, 738 North Chestnut Street

The Bushwhackers made sarcastic remarks about "Happy Kansas", as they led the Judy brothers away after destroying the house. Their lifeless bodies were found not far from the house the next morning. John Judy had been shot five times; his brother, James, shot three times. Both John and James Judy are buried in the Olathe Cemetery.

We have historical accounts of the Cook and Judy brothers'

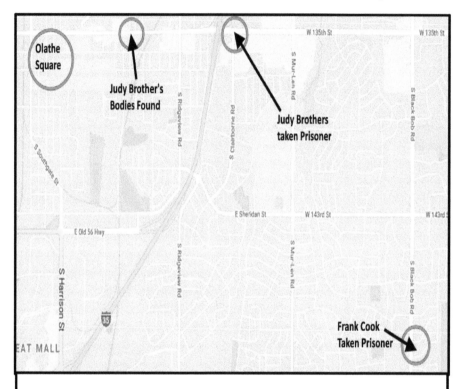

Figure 86: Locations on this map are estimated based on research and may not the exact location of events.

murders. In addition to these killings, Lieutenant Gregg, in his account, reports that Quantrill's men had killed seven other men on their way to Olathe saying, "before we reached Olathe, we had killed ten men, of most of whom were known to our men" (Connelley 157).

Quantrill and his 140 men arrived on the outskirts of Olathe around midnight on Sunday morning, September 7th. At the Mill Creek bridge over Sante Fe Street, Quantrill sent 60 of his men to surround the town, establishing pickets around the entire town. These men were given orders to "shoot anyone who tries to escape" the net that had been placed around Olathe. The rest of the men split into two groups; one group entering the town on the "Old Trail", on the south side of the square, while the rest entered the square on the north side via Sante Fe Street.

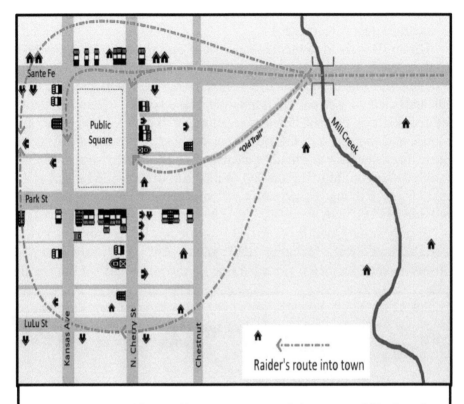

Figure 87: Quantrill sent 60 men to surround the town, while the others rode into the public square, one group from the south via the "Old Trail" and the other from the north via Sante Fe Street.

The night was clear and cloudless with a full moon that lit everything up like it was daylight. Quantrill's Raiders, after encircling the town, were likely to have entered the town square from several different directions. There are eyewitness accounts that have the Bushwhackers initially entering the square from both the north and south side of Cherry Street. This inconsistency can likely be attributed to the fact that the marauders were split up and coming to the square in different groups. To eyewitnesses, it probably appeared that they were coming from everywhere. At first some of the townsfolk, a handful of whom were still enjoying a lively Saturday night drinking at the Star Saloon, mistook the riders for a Union cavalry company. The fact that many of the raiders would have been wearing stolen federal uniforms probably led to this assumption.   William Roy, the Olathe Post Adjutant, noticed the riders and hailed them, "Is this Captain Harvey's Command?" The Bushwhackers responded, "Yes" and then proceeded to take the square (Kamberg).

Hiram Blanchard, a businessman from Spring Hill, was enjoying a drink in the Star Saloon on the east side of the square when Quantrill and men rode into town. Once he realized what was happening, he went out and tried to get on his horse and leave town. Quantrill's men informed Hiram that the horse now belonged to them. Blanchard drew a knife and tried to stab the Bushwhacker holding his horse. Another Bushwhacker who was standing nearby shot Blanchard with a double-barreled shotgun, blowing the top of his head off. While he was lying near his horse dying, Blanchard was "stripped of all clothing save shirt and drawers" (Thavis).

Shortly after Quantrill's arrival into the square, a group of newly recruited soldiers, realizing the town was being overrun by Bushwhackers, formed a skirmish line on the south side of the square

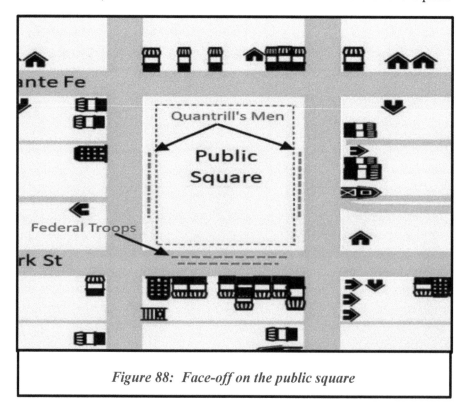

Figure 88: Face-off on the public square

on Park Street. Quantrill ordered his men to tie their horses to the fence that surrounded the courthouse square, stand behind the horses and aim their pistols at the soldiers. Quantrill shouted at the soldiers that if they surrendered, no harm would come to them. Only one soldier, Patrick Bean, (most accounts from the time make note that Bean was an "Irishman") did not surrender, and he was quickly shot and killed. The soldiers were taken prisoner and herded into the public square where they could be dealt with. The fence around the public square made it an ideal place to "corral" the prisoners. The Bushwhackers called the square, the "bullpen" (Thavis).

Sources vary as to whether these defenders of Olathe were federal soldiers or a militia company that was in Olathe. We know for sure that there was a recruiting station in Olathe, run by J.E. Hayes from which a new rifle company, the Twelfth Kansas regiment, Company A, was leaving from Olathe the next morning. For this reason, it seems logical that these soldiers were more likely federal recruits from the new rifle company.

Quantrill noticed several young men standing outside the courthouse and soon learned that this building, on the south side of the square, was being used for temporary housing for new recruits. Everyone inside the courthouse was ordered out. Several young recruits filed out, most of them unarmed (Wood 112). After most of the soldiers had left the courthouse, a group of guerrillas stormed the building to search and make sure the building was empty. As they rushed up the stairs, a recruit by the name of Phillip Wiggins, caught one of the Bushwhackers by the throat and took his pistol away and was in the process of choking him when he was shot in the head by another guerilla.

The number of soldiers in the initial skirmish line and the number in the building present a discrepancy when reviewing the historic accounts. Several of the more recent accounts put the number of soldiers at around 125. This number is likely taken from William Gregg's manuscript which lists that number in the skirmish line. However, I have found other accounts, that mention 125 men in the skirmish and then another 100 that filed out of the courthouse. Both of these numbers are likely too high. Research has uncovered multiple eyewitness accounts which puts the actual number of soldiers eventually confined to the bullpen and later marched out of town at approximately 25. This smaller number makes more sense when you consider that these men would have been housed in just a few small buildings around the square and it is highly unlikely that these buildings could have housed between 125 and 225 men. It also makes the initial surrender make more sense if only 15 – 20 men made up the federal skirmish line and were faced with over 80 guns around the public square. A headcount of 25 soldiers seems to be a much more realistic number and is confirmed by Lieutenant William Pellet, a recruiting officer and eventual Mayor of Olathe. He says in his account, that 25 of his men were confined in the bullpen (Blair, 1915 107). This smaller number is also confirmed by other primary sources including the *Chicago Tribune*, dated September 13, 1862, as well as Francis R. Morrison's work in *Sharing Memories*.

As the guerrillas searched the buildings in the town, they came upon Josiah Skinner, an 18-year-old recruit who was still in bed upstairs in a building that was being used as the Presbyterian Church on East Park Street, just off the square. Skinner would not respond to the order to get up and get out of the building. Whether Skinner really did not hear

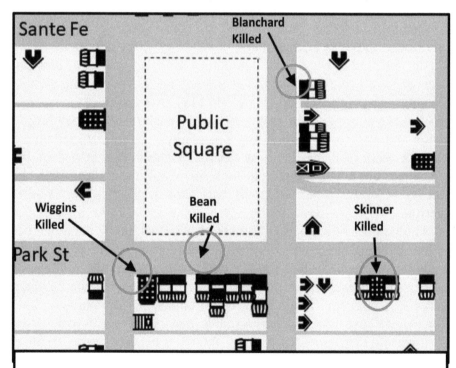

Figure 89: Hiram Blanchard was killed just outside of the Star Saloon. Phillip Wiggins was killed on the stairs of the courthouse. Josiah Skinner was killed in the Presbyterian Church building.

the order, or was just trying to fake being asleep, we will never know. What we do know is that the raiders shot Skinner in the abdomen, a wound from which he would die a few days later.

After the soldiers in the skirmish line surrendered and the public square was under control, Quantrill and his men went house to house in the surrounding blocks, ordering all men into the public square. Quantrill addressed all the civilians and soldiers who had been gathered in the square, and told them, "We're just here to take ammunition, horses and supplies. Nobody else will get hurt if you co-operate. But if a single one of my men is harmed, we'll burn the town" (Wood). The *Oskaloosa Independent* described the rest of the night in this way, "From that time until he [Quantrill] left at an early hour in the morning, he and his men were engaged in the work of murder, plunder and devastation" (1862). The paper uses a bit of poetic license here as there were no more killings after this point in the evening.

Olathe citizen, Alex Rottman described the bullpen in this way:

> *Upon reaching the square, I found that I was not the only prisoner – they having already some 30 or 40 [prisoners] and still they came. I could think of nothing like it, except the driving in and corralling of sheep" (Goodrich, Black Flag 39).*

Multiple accounts report that there were as many as 50 civilian men held in the town square in addition to the approximately 25 soldiers. Women were not forced into the square and no women were physically harmed in the raid. Quantrill throughout his short career was very adamant with his men that his command would never harm women and his men generally followed those orders. One of Quantrill's men, James Campbell recalled Quantrill's orders regarding women this way:

> *Quantrill gave orders that any member of his troop who insulted a woman should be shot. He said to us, "No matter how much a woman may abuse you, take her abuse. Let her talk and scold but say nothing to her in resentment. We are fighting men, not women. No provocation will excuse an insult or back-talk to a woman."*
> *(Goodrich, Black Flag 36)*

According to the *Oskaloosa Independent*, the first places ransacked were the stores that surrounded the town square. S. F. Hill, whose store was on the west side of the square, saw his store plundered and cleaned out, with the Bushwhackers taking about $900 worth of cash and goods. William Pellet's and Frederik Hoff's stores on the south side of the square were ransacked with the looters taking approximately $2,000 worth of goods. C.M. Ott's bakery and grocery, on the north side of the square, was also cleaned out.

Hoff was a prisoner in the "bullpen" when his wife came out of his store calling for him to come back and save the merchandise in the store from the looters. Hoff tried to leave the bullpen to go back to his store but was told by the guerrillas guarding the prisoners to stay where he was. Indignantly he ignored the orders and kept going toward his store at which point he was leveled by a musket blow to the head (Milhoan 1). Many years after the raid, an eyewitness account given by J.H. Milhoan, Constable of Olathe at the time of the raid, lists Mr. Hoff's name as "A.M. Hoff" and says that he owned a store on the west side of the square. Research has turned up no record of an "A.M. Hoff" and thus no record of he and his wife owning a store on the west side. Multiple primary sources confirm that "Frederik Hoff" was a resident at the time and did own a store on the south side of the square. (See advertisement in the previous chapter) While there is no way to know for sure, this author believes that A.M. Hoff is a misprint or a misremembrance and that he and Frederik Hoff are the same person.

There were two newspapers in town, the *Olathe Herald* and the *Olathe Mirror*. The Herald was generally considered to be a pro-southern paper while the *Mirror* was an anti-slavery paper. Local history says that the Bushwhackers destroyed all equipment at the *Herald* first, mistakenly thinking it was the *Mirror*. Once they realized their mistake, they immediately went to the offices of the *Olathe Mirror* and repeated the same type of destruction at that location. Days later, John Francis, editor of the *Olathe Mirror* wrote, "My ruin financially is complete. The labor of years, and my future hopes – gone" (Goodrich, Black Flag 39).

Quantrill's men also went into the courthouse and destroyed all the city records stored in that building by ripping them into shreds. On the west side of the square, guerrillas noticed a Union flag flying over J.E. Hayes recruiting office. (The location of this office is unknown; it may have been one of the two buildings on Kansas Avenue, just to the north of the Turpin House.) The guerrillas yelled, to nobody in particular, "Take down that flag, God damn you, take down that flag or we will shoot you." No one attempted to take down the flag and it was then shot full of holes, torn down and trampled in the dust (Hermon 2). At one point in the plundering of the town, including all the private residences, the guerrillas ran out of wagons which were going to be used to carry all the stolen loot back to Missouri. Quantrill dispatched men to go outside the encircled town to find more wagons and teams to pull them.

One of those farms on the outskirts of town that the Bush-whackers visited was the Mahaffie farm, which was a regular stop on the Sante Fe trail and one of the largest farms in the Olathe area. Upon their arrival at the Mahaffie farm, about one-mile northeast of the downtown, the

Figure 90: The Mahaffie House and Farm have been preserved and are a National Historic Site. www.Mahaffie.org

Bushwhackers found the doors un-locked and wide open. According to Phil Campbell, historic programs coordinator of Mahaffie Stagecoach Stop and Farm Historic Site, "Lucinda Mahaffie left the front door wide open. She also opened all the kitchen cupboards and left the kitchen door ajar." The idea was that if she could draw the looters attention to certain things, they might leave other things alone. Lucinda also sent her children to chase the horses to the very back of the farm in the hopes that the guerrillas would not see them (Kamberg).

The guerrillas searched and looted all the private residences in the town. They went a little easier on the households that were known to be sympathetic to the Confederacy, but the only buildings that escaped the plunder were the Turpin House on the west side of the square and the residence of Judge Campbell, on the southeast corner of the square. Both the Judge and the Turpin family were known as Southern Sympathizers. While in the private residences, the raiders would take anything that they desired or looked useful. Anything they didn't want, they would destroy; smashing furniture and breaking windows and doors. They would also take any pictures of young girls. There is no evidence as to why Quantrill's men would take these pictures but the taking of these images is consistent in reports of other raids by Quantrill's men.

According to the author's family history, Quantrill and his men stopped at the C.M. Ott home, which was located on Sante Fe Street, just off the square on the southeast corner of Cherry and Sante Fe streets. Quantrill ordered Mrs. Justine Ott, to prepare breakfast for himself and 30 of his men, telling her that they would return for breakfast when their work was done. Mrs. Ott prepared a meal of ham, eggs, biscuits and coffee. Only fifteen men, Quantrill not among them, showed up to eat the meal a few hours later. The men that did come were noisy and stole everything that was loose, including $20.25 in cash (Jones).

Figure 91: Justine Ott, wife of C.M. Ott, was ordered to prepare breakfast for Quantrill and his men.

There is another account of the raid, taken from a high school paper written in 1929 that has this breakfast story being replayed for another Olathe family, Mr. and Mrs. Noteman. Both stories may be true as this breakfast request is not uncommon on other guerrilla raids and the expectation of one family to feed 140 men is not realistic. It is also possible that over time the stories have morphed and been claimed by more than one family historian. That said, the Noteman story comes from a source that is riddled with incorrect facts and, other than this mention was not used in this work due to the factual issues with that source.

While his men were looting the town, Quantrill noted an acquaintance from Paola, Judge E.W. Robinson, in the corral. He asked Robinson to come over and sit on the fence and talk for a while. Robinson recalls,

During this conversation, I addressed him as Bill – he very politely requested me to address him as Captain Quantrill and took from his pocket and showed me what he claimed was a commission from the Confederate Government, but I did not read it. Being an old acquaintance, and having no grudge against me, he treated me kindly. (Leslie 145)

Another of Olathe's judges, J.P. Campbell experienced a close call during the raid. Campbell was a known Southern Sympathizer and was acquainted with Quantrill prior to the raid. Quantrill told Campbell to stay close to him and he would make sure that his horse, taken by a Bushwhacker, would be returned to him before the raiders left town. Campbell had gone to the Turpin house where he overheard a conversation about Mrs. Turpin's message to the Bushwhackers about the town's defenses. Realizing that the Judge had overheard the conversation and that his knowledge may be harmful to Mrs. Turpin, they decided they needed to eliminate Campbell. Mrs. Turpin asked them not to kill him in her house. While escorting the judge out of the house for his execution, they ran into another group of Bushwhackers. Judge Campbell used this as a distraction and ran south hiding in the middle of a small group of women huddled just off the street. When asked if they had seen him, the women covered for the judge and told his pursuers that he had gone south down the street, thus saving his life.

After the searching of all the houses was complete, the prisoners in the town square were divided up with the soldiers on one side of the square and civilians on the other. The soldiers were given strict orders not to try and go over to the civilian side of the bullpen. John Giffin, owner of the Olathe Herald Newspaper, annoyed Quantrill by moving around too much during the division of soldiers and civilians. Quantrill yelled at Giffin, "Get over there you red- headed hound!". Giffin bowed deeply and replied, "Auburn, if you please sir." Quantrill laughed and said, "You're all right, get over there where you belong" (Morrison 36). Remember that the Olathe Herald was the Southern Sympathizing paper so Giffin may have had a bit more leeway than might have been shown to other civilians. All the prisoners, both soldiers and civilians were stripped of their clothes down to their underwear. Clothing was always in short supply for the guerilla bands during this period. It was common that these bands would take clothing from towns that were sacked.

From the time Quantrill read about Perry Hoy's execution, we know that at least ten men were killed in direct response to that act; Lieutenant Copeland, the two Union prisoners at Woodsmall's camp, Frank Cook, John and James Judy, Hiram Blanchard, Phillip Wiggins, Patrick Bean and Josiah Skinner. Other accounts put the death toll anywhere from twelve to twenty men. Author Albert Castel claims that twelve men were killed in Olathe alone, however, this author finds no evidence to support that number. Recall that Gregg's firsthand account contends that ten men were killed on the way to Olathe and then four killed in Olathe, for a total of 14 deaths. What is the exact number? We will likely never know. A minimum of ten men lost their lives in response to Perry's Hoy's execution. Just as Quantrill had promised.

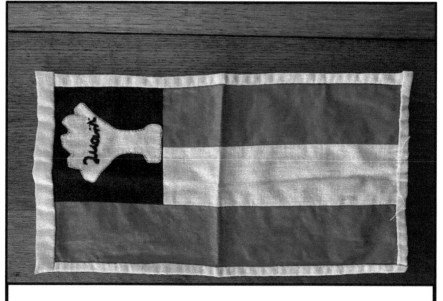

Figure 92: The flag in above, a replica created by Mary Talbot, is reported to have been dropped by one of Quantrill's men during the raid. The flag is small, 7 x 13 inches. The purpose of the flag is unknown. Some historians think it was a "regimental flag", while others think it may have been a "Bible Flag" commonly used to mark passages in the Bible. Quantrill was not known to fly any type of regimental flag, which makes the "Bible Flag" a more plausible explanation. The palmetto tree in the upper right-hand corner was a common Confederate symbol of the times. Image courtesy of Robert Courtney.

At around seven the next morning, Sunday, September 7th, Quantrill ordered his men to head south toward Spring Hill, Kansas. The procession out of Olathe included Quantrill's men, 13 wagons full of plunder, somewhere between 35 and 50 horses, and the federal soldiers, on foot, wearing only their underwear. The civilians who had been held in the bullpen had been released. On their way out of town, the *Oskaloosa Independent* reports that Quantrill said that he was headed to Paola and "would not rest until he had laid the border in ruin". Lieutenant William Pellet, a local recruiting officer and the man in command of the recruits, was afforded the courtesy of a horse to ride on the trip out of town. The horse was provided to him by former Olathe resident and current guerrilla, Cliff Turpin, who likely knew Pellet from his time in Olathe.

A few miles out of town another Bushwhacker approached Pellet and encouraged him to run away calling him a "little Yankee schoolmaster runt." Wisely, the small in stature Pellet, declined the offer knowing he would be shot as soon as he tried to escape.

Before the caravan arrived in Spring Hill, word was received that there were a large number of Union soldiers in Spring Hill. Hearing this news, Quantrill turned due east and marched the prisoners to Squiresville, a small town about six miles southeast of Olathe, where they stopped to rest. His men ate breakfast after forcing all the prisoners into a small storeroom. (The fact that all the soldiers were confined in a single storeroom solidifies the logic that there were likely around 25 soldiers, rather than over 125)

After breakfast, Quantrill lined all the prisoners up in front of him and said, "For the last half hour I have been doing something I never did before. I have been making up my mind whether to shoot you or not." He then informed them that he had decided not to shoot them if they would take an oath promising not to take up arms against the Confederacy (Thavis). While the oath was being administered, two men were pulled out of the group and pushed to a spot apart from the other soldiers. John Dunn and A. P. Trahern were not administered the oath and were not released with the other prisoners. Instead, they were forced to drive a wagon with the guerrillas back to Missouri. Trahern was suspected of being with Jennison's Jayhawkers when they sacked Harrisonville earlier in the year. Dunn was likely suspected of a similar act, but no record exists of why he might have been chosen. Both

Trahern and Dunn denied these accusations, but their protestations fell on deaf ears.

Once the oath was administered to the prisoners and their leaders, they were released with directions to run back to Olathe. Quantrill is reported to have told them to leave and go home and "be good boys"

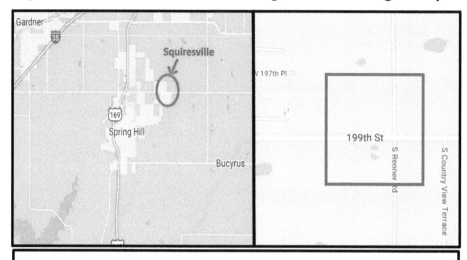

Figure 93: Squiresville, Kansas, which no longer exists, was located at what is now the intersection of 199th Street and Renner Road on the outskirts of Spring Hill, Kansas.

(Castel). The soldiers, excluding Dunn and Trahern, turned and ran toward Olathe, unsure if they would be shot in the back as they left for home or not. True to his word, Quantrill let them go and they reached Olathe around noon, hungry and tired.

Late in the afternoon on Monday, November 8th, the Bushwhackers reached the woods around the Grand River, near present-day Peculiar, Missouri, where they made camp. They had only been in the woods for a little while when the residents from that part of Cass County began arriving with food and drink for the weary raiders. Thavis, in his article written 25 years later in the Olathe Herald, surmises that the timing of the arrival of these provisions tells us that this rendezvous was preplanned although there is no evidence to support this claim. This show of support of Quantrill and his raiders by the locals clearly indicates the division on the border and how the state line divided two very different opinions of the guerrillas and their methods. On the Missouri side, Quantrill and his men were viewed as warriors and protectors doing their job as soldiers in a war. On the Kansas side of the line, these same men were viewed as cutthroats, thieves and murderers.

While camped near the Grand River, Trahern and Dunn were tied to a wagon wheel overnight. The fact that these two men had not been

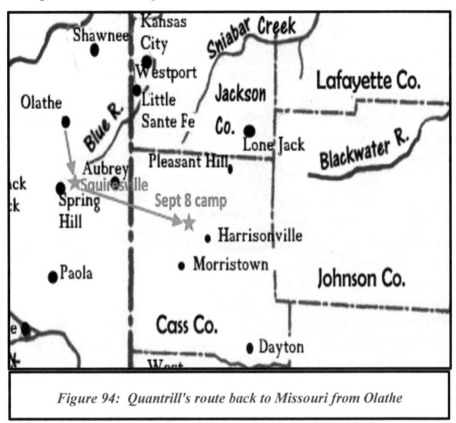

Figure 94: Quantrill's route back to Missouri from Olathe

released increased the pressure, and thus the urgency, on the part of the Federal Army and the Kansas Militia in the Olathe area to rescue them. To accomplish this, John G. Jackson, a Squiresville resident and known Southern Sympathizer was "enlisted", under threat of death, to go and speak with Quantrill and secure the prisoners' release. Mr. Jackson, having no real choice, agreed and reached the Quantrill campsite in the very early morning hours on Tuesday, November 9th. The overnight trip was not necessary because when Jackson arrived at the Bushwhacker's camp, Quantrill was nowhere to be found. Quantrill rarely camped with his men. Rather, it was his habit to sleep in secluded spots where nobody, not even his men, knew where he was. This "habit" was a safeguard against a surprise attack or treachery from inside his command.

Quantrill arrived back in camp later that day and listened to Jackson detail the events of the previous evening and the consequences to himself [Jackson] if Dunn and Trahern were not released. It is reported that Quantrill felt that the life of one "Southern Sympathizer", Jackson, was more valuable than the lives of the two Union men. He released Dunn and Trahern, whose execution was likely planned for that morning. When he returned to Olathe, Trahern would describe his captor this way:

Quantrill had his men thoroughly disciplined and his orders were obeyed with alacrity (enthusiasm) when or wherever given. Occasionally a scout would come excitedly to him and report that a body of men had been seen or that something alarming had happened. Quantrill unconcerned apparently, would answer "See who they are, " or "see that they do not come too close" and ride on as cool and calm as if danger to him was unknown. (Milhoan 5)

In her letter to Horace Hickock, older brother of the man who would eventually be known as "Wild Bill Hickock", Nancy Grace Potter, a 21-year-old woman who witnessed the raid on Olathe, described the scene this way, "…the town the next day looked like a demolished beehive with the bees flying around, but did not think it worthwhile to save what was left" (Herman 3).

Dr. Thomas Hamil in a letter to Major General Curtis on November 6, 1862, describes the Olathe Raid like this:

I was in Olathe when Quantrill came there; he took everything of wearing apparel and all the horses that he could get; he took all of my clothes, a good horse, and a fine gold watch; but we did not care for being robbed, if he had not killed our citizens in cold blood, taking our best citizens from the bosom of their families and shooting them down like so many hogs (Kamberg).

There was significant public pressure after the Olathe Raid on the federal authorities to catch Quantrill and protect the border towns. Colonel John Burris was dispatched immediately to bring Quantrill and his men to justice. Burris was an Olathe resident and attorney who had maintained an office next to the courthouse before the war. Once the war began, Burris rode as a sergeant with Lane's Brigade and was eventually promoted to Lieutenant Colonel in the Tenth Kansas

Volunteer Infantry. Over the next two weeks, Colonel Burris and his
men chased Quantrill through Jackson, Cass, Johnson and Lafayette
counties in Missouri. Typical of guerrilla warfare, Burris and his men
were unable to force Quantrill into a formal engagement. In his "after-
action report" Burris commented that he was "unable to bring on an
engagement, other than the occasional picket skirmish." Burris and his
command finally got their chance on September 19th, five miles north
of the Cass County town of Pleasant Hill.

Burris engaged Quantrill's men with significant gunfire for about
ten minutes before the guerrillas broke and fled. Two guerrillas were
killed in this short battle, one federal soldier was killed and three were
wounded. The federal troops followed the fleeing guerrillas for about
two miles at which time the guerrillas entered the woods and scattered
into many directions making them impossible to follow. Upon entering
the woods, the guerrillas abandoned many of the wagons carrying the
spoils taken from Olathe. In his report, Colonel Burris lists the
following items that were recovered at this time:

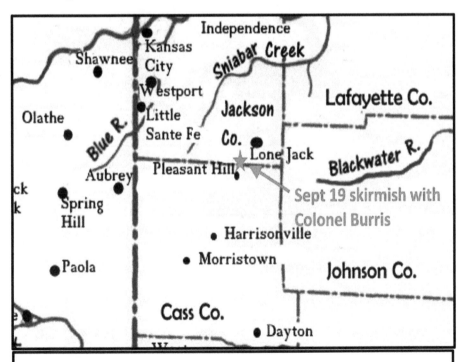

Figure 95: Quantrill and Lieutenant Colonel Burris skirmished 5 miles
north of Pleasant Hill, Missouri, on September 19, 1862.

One hundred stand of arms, 10,000 rounds of ammunition, 100 horses, 5 wagons, a number of tents and other camp equipage; also, a considerable quantity of dry goods, groceries which had been stolen from the people in Olathe.

Burris also notes in his report that, while in Missouri, he and his men burned the homes, outbuildings, grain, etc. of farms where the guerrillas had been "known to haunt" (Official report of General Burris 1862).

With another unsuccessful attempt to capture Quantrill and his men, the Kansas papers had plenty to say regarding the job that the federal authorities had done protecting Kansan border towns and their residents. The Chicago Tribune reported:

The people of Kansas residing on the border are not only excited but mad. The government affords no protection and the Kansas troops who are used to border warfare, are in Mississippi. Everybody interested in having the state protected from the robbers, [should] express their desire for the return of Colonel Jennison's old regiment, the 7th Kansas. This regiment is made up in part of men who fought the border ruffians under "old John Brown" and General Lane in 56 and 57 and understand guerrilla warfare." (Chicago Tribune, Sept 13, 1862)

A few days after the raid, on September 11, The Lawrence *Western Home Journal* had this warning for other border towns after the Olathe Raid,

While we trust that General Blunt will take measures to prevent a recurrence of such attacks upon our border towns, it will not do for the people to depend on him. They must organize home guards for their own defense and must keep out nightly guards to prevent surprise. Had there been a well-organized and drilled company of fifty men in Olathe with a proper guard out, the town could never have been taken by any guerrilla force likely to venture even so short a distance of that into Kansas. Let our other towns take warning. The success of the raid will encourage similar ones on a bolder scale." (Kansas Invaded 2)

Ironically, the *Western Journal* was printed in Lawrence, Kansas, a town that would undergo a much more devastating raid by Quantrill's Raiders a mere 12 months later. Failing to take the advice of its newspaper cost the city of Lawrence dearly, as it was totally unprepared for the attack that would destroy their city in August of 1863.

The Sacking of Lawrence

One cannot write about William Quantrill and not mention the Raid on Lawrence. This incident is why Quantrill is famous and the primary event that people think of when considering the Border War. Any study of the man and the era would not be complete without mentioning the event. There are volumes of work that go into extreme detail on this event and I am not going to try and recreate that as it has already been done and is not the focus of this work. What follows is a brief summary of the event so a reader with limited knowledge of the raid can at least get a feel for what happened on that fateful summer day. The Raid of Lawrence occurred on August 21, 1863 and was essentially the climax of the Border War. In the national consciousness, all other incidents pale in comparison to this one event. I encourage anyone who wants more detail on the Lawrence Massacre to investigate the resources in the bibliography for more information about what remains the most infamous, historical event in the history of the State of Kansas.

After Olathe, Quantrill and his men remained active on the Kansas side of the border. During the period between October 1862 and June 1863, Lane and Jennison had been neutralized by Union authorities due to the bad press their tactics had generated. Jennison had been removed from command and Lane had been called back east to play Senator for a while. Jayhawkers still occupied and raided western Missouri but not on the large scale that the region had seen in late 1862. Quantrill and his Bushwhackers took advantage of this respite to exact some revenge in the Kansas border counties. After the Olathe Raid, Quantrill and other Bushwhacker leaders would raid the Kansas towns of Shawnee, Spring Hill and Council Grove, as well as leading raids on travelers on the Sante Fe Trail.

From the beginning of the Bleeding Kansas era through the end of the Civil War, Lawrence was always a target for Pro-Southern guerillas. The town was largely settled by abolitionists from the east. During the Bleeding Kansas era, it was where much of the rhetoric and the "noise" about making Kansas a free-state originated. As an abolitionist town, Lawrence was also known to be very active in the Underground Railroad, as well as being the home of Missouri's number one enemy, James Lane. If you were going to raid a town in Kansas, Lawrence was the big prize. If you wanted to make a splash for the Confederacy, Lawrence was the ideal target.

Figure 96: Lawrence, Kansas is located approximately 40 miles west of Kansas City.

While many Missourians, Quantrill's men included, hated the people of Lawrence, the collapse of the women's prison in Kansas City is often cited as the reason that Quantrill and his lieutenants decided to raid Lawrence. It was the policy of General Thomas Ewing to arrest women relatives of men who were known to ride with a Bushwhacker unit. This policy included sisters, wives, mothers and any other female relative of these men.

Figure 97: Historic Marker across the street from the site of the women's prison collapse. The T-Mobile Center now sits where the prison stood on the day of the collapse.

The prison, which was located at 1425 Grand Avenue in Kansas City, was reported to have been structurally weakened by the Union soldiers who were guarding it. Some reports say that the soldiers were weakening the building on purpose while other reports say they were taking the wood from the structure for firewood. Regardless, the foundation of the building was weakened significantly and collapsed at 2 pm on Friday, August 14, 1863. Several women were killed, and many others were injured. Josephine Anderson, the sister of "Bloody Bill" Anderson, was one of the women killed in the collapse. Most of the men who rode with Quantrill had relatives or knew women who were either killed or injured in the collapse. While the prison collapse may have given Quantrill a rallying cry, he and his men had been discussing raiding Lawrence well before the prison collapse.

The collapse of the prison sent the Missouri guerillas into a frenzy. Someone needed to pay for what the Union Army had done to their womenfolk. To add fuel to the fire, four days later on August 18th, General Ewing, the Commander of the District of the Border, issued Order Number 10. This order decreed that all family members of any man who was riding with the guerillas were officially banished from the state and would need to leave immediately. It's almost as if Ewing was daring the Bushwhackers to take some retaliatory action. Quantrill and his men accepted the challenge and raided the city of Lawrence on the morning of August 21st, seven days after the collapse of the women's prison.

When Quantrill and his men left Lawrence, 180 men and boys had been killed, the majority of the town was burned, and most items of value had been taken. Jim Lane had survived by escaping into a cornfield behind his house in his pajamas and hiding in a ravine. The death toll of the Lawrence Raid far exceeded any single event by either Jayhawkers or Bushwhackers up to this point in the Border War. While no women were harmed, there are reports of the Bushwhackers talking and acting crudely to the women that were trying to save their property and protect their husbands and sons.

The attack on Lawrence brought even more national media attention to the situation on the Missouri/Kansas border and, as you would expect, the opposing sides covered the event with very different viewpoints. In their August 24, 1863 edition, The *New York Daily Times* had this to say;

Quantrill's massacre at Lawrence is almost enough to curdle the blood with horror. In the history of the war thus far, full as it has been of dreadful scenes, there has been no such diabolical work as this indiscriminate slaughter of peaceful villagers. . .. We find it impossible to believe that men who have ever borne the name of American can have been transformed . . . into such fiends incarnate . . . It is a calamity of the most heartrending kind—an atrocity of unspeakable character. (August 24, 1863)

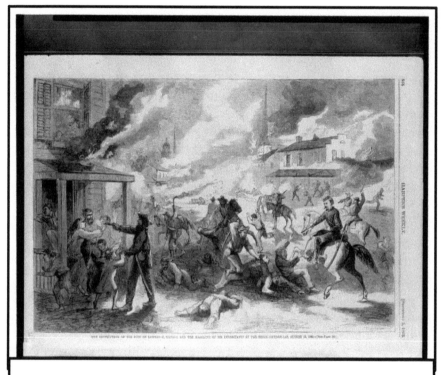

Figure 98: Drawing depicting the Raid of Lawrence printed in Harper's Weekly on September 5, 1863. Image courtesy of the Library of Congress

Not surprisingly, southern papers took a different view. The *Charleston Mercury* called the raid, "A perfect success", while the Richmond *Examiner* said, "The expedition to Lawrence was a gallant and perfectly fair blow at the enemy . . . as the population of Kansas is malignant and scoundrelly beyond description" (Goodrich, Black Flag 96).

Figure 99: Raid of Lawrence. Image courtesy of Kansas State Historical Society

Quantrill and his men would leave Lawrence and make their way back to Missouri dodging the federal troops under the command of General Thomas Ewing, who had been raised to pursue them. Ewing himself would commend Quantrill for his skillful use of his best men to ride at the rear of his column to delay Ewing and his men while the main column moved east. This "rear guard" would attack the federal forces with just enough vigor to force them to stop and form up into battle formation. Then they would quickly ride away at such a speed that they were impossible to pursue. This tactic allowed Quantrill and his entire force to get safely back to the Missouri woodlands within 24 hours of the attack. The Bushwhackers would only lose one man during the raid and a small number more on the retreat, before evaporating into the Missouri countryside (Goodrich, Black Flag, 95).

Order Number 11

The sacking of Lawrence infuriated Kansans and Missouri military leaders. Among those leaders was Jim Lane, who had barely escaped death during the raid. Lane blamed the lack of preparedness for the raid on General Thomas Ewing, the Commander of The District of the Border. Lane and Ewing met in a small cabin days after the raid where together they drafted a document which would eventually become known as "Order Number 11". As the two men left the cabin, Lane yelled to Ewing and said, "You are a dead dog, if you fail to issue that order" (Leslie 258). Order Number 11 was issued on August 25, 1863, four days after the raid on Lawrence.

Order Number 11 mandated that all residents in Jackson, Cass, Bates and the northern part of Vernon counties, except those citizens who lived within one mile of a designated military station, were to vacate their homes and relocate out of the district. If the citizens could prove their loyalty to the satisfaction of the leader of one of the military stations, they would receive permission to reside at the station. The designated military stations were located in Harrisonville, Pleasant Hill, Hickman Mills, Independence and the Kaw River area which included Kansas City and Westport. The remainder of the named counties, totaling approximately 2,200 acres, were to be completely vacated by September 9th, 15 days from the passing of the order. All grain and other crops, in the field or barns, would be confiscated and become the property of the federal authorities. This order applied to citizens on both sides of the war effort. It did not matter where your loyalties lied. You had to leave your home.

Remember, this was 1863 and news did not travel as fast as it does today. Some of the residents of the area, now mostly women, children and senior or invalid men, did not find out about the order until the "enforcers" showed up at their door ready to burn their homes and farms to the ground.

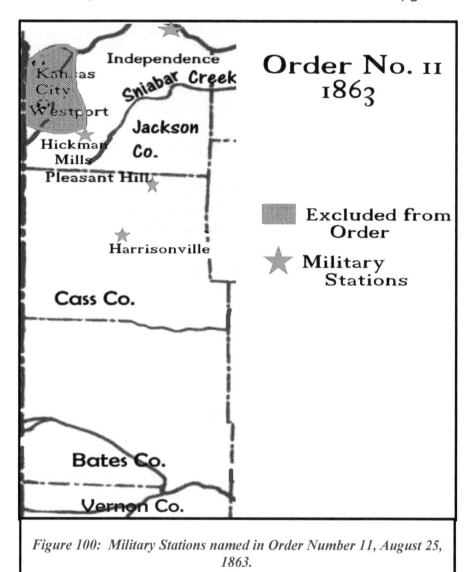

Figure 100: Military Stations named in Order Number 11, August 25, 1863.

Most of the citizens who still resided in the area had no means with which to transport their belongings from their homes. Over the past several years of border strife, their good horses and wagons had been confiscated by either the Jayhawkers, Red Legs, Bushwhackers or the Union Army. Most were left only with milk cows and old animals that would struggle to pull a wagon. Wagons were also in short supply as those too had been confiscated to haul booty back to Kansas. There are reports that evicted residents would put wheels on anything that they could make into a makeshift wagon to at least try and take some of their belongings with them. Many of these hastily cobbled together wagons had to be pulled by hand.

Pro-Union Kansas City politician and painter, George Caleb Bingham, cornered General Ewing and demanded that he rescind the order which he called "stupid and outrageous". Bingham continued to berate Ewing saying:

I will say now, and continue to say that Order Number Eleven is nothing but a revenge move on your part to pacify the people of Kansas who, you hope, someday after the war may have an opportunity to vote for you in preference to Jim Lane. . . . If you persist in executing this order, I shall make you infamous with my pen and brush so far as I am able. (Schultz 247)

Figure 101: George Caleb Bingham's "Martial Law", depicts a Kansas Red Leg forcing Missouri residents out of their homes. It also shows many homes burning in the background. Image courtesy of the State Historical Society of Missouri, Art Collection

Bingham would follow through on his threat by creating the famous painting titled, "Martial Law". In the painting, Ewing is shown on a horse evicting women and children from homes with burning homesteads filling the landscape. Years later, in 1877, Bingham paraded the painting through Ohio where Ewing was running for Governor. The failed gubernatorial bid was the end of Ewing's political career.

General Ewing brought Charles "Doc" Jennison out of "retirement" to command the Kansas 15th Cavalry and empowered this unit to oversee the Order Number 11 region. As would be expected, given Jennison's past, his command was comprised of men of questionable character. Goodrich, quoting a sergeant in the Kansas 15th, says that the unit was made up of "thieves, robbers and murderers" who had been recruited out of the "penitentiaries, jails and guardhouses" (Goodrich, Black Flag 155). Jennison's men were given free rein to terrorize anyone left in the district. They would travel from farm to farm, taking what spoils they could find before forcing the families out of their homes, which were then burned to the ground. The landscape was said to be one of ashes and cinders remaining around lone chimneys that were the only remnants of the now destroyed family homes. There are reports of eyewitnesses looking out over the landscape and seeing as many as 50 homes burning within sight. The large number of these smoldering homes earned the area the nickname of the "Burnt District". The *Oskaloosa Independent* described the devastation this way:

> *The border counties of Missouri have become almost as desolate in appearance as before the soil was trod by the white man. Not a man, woman or child is to be seen in the country to which Order Number 11 applies. . .. Chimneys mark the spot where once stood costly farmhouses, cattle and hogs are fast destroying large fields of corn, prairie fires are burning up miles of good fencing every day or two, and turn which way you will, everything denotes a state of utter desolation and ruin. (October 10, 1863)*

Late August and early September was western Missouri is hot and dry. The refugees who were leaving their homes were walking down dusty roads that had not seen rain in quite some time. The lines on the roads out of the district were filled for miles with a continuous line of weary refugees trying to get out of the area. Some went south, some went north to the Missouri River. The citizens with money might be able to secure passage on a boat to go either north to St. Joseph or east to Lexington or Boonville. Most were destitute, carrying all their worldly belongings on their backs as they walked the dust-filled roads.

Many of these evictees had no idea where they were going, they just knew that they had to leave.

The sheer number of refugees caused problems for surrounding counties as well. Ray, Clay and Lafayette Counties were not prepared for the large influx of refugees. Remember that these people, many now clothed only in rags, had no food, shelter or money. The burden fell upon these destinations to try and figure out what to do with them. Eventually, both Clay and Ray Counties, on the north side of the Missouri River, closed their counties to all refugees from the district. It is estimated that over 20,000 residents left the Burnt District as a result of Order Number 11. While it is impossible to know exactly how many left or how many died because of the hardships created due to the order, unofficial records state that Cass County had 10,000 residents on the day that Order Number 11 was enacted and by September 9th, 15 days later, the count was fewer than 600 (Leslie 260).

Figure 102: Burnt District Monument, located in Harrisonville, Missouri

Bates County was wiped out by the order. Every single town in that county simply disappeared. West Point, the county's largest prewar border town, never returned and was simply wiped off the map. In Cass County, only a small number of people in Harrisonville and Pleasant Hill remained. In Jackson County, only Hickman Mills, Kansas City, Independence and Westport remained in existence, while the rest of the county became a barren wasteland (Rafiner 237). Author Thomas Goodrich, calls Order Number 11, "the harshest act of the U.S. Government against its own people in American History" (Gilmore,

Red Legs 100), while author Tom Rafiner calls it one of "America's lowest moments" (Rafiner 212).

In the end, Order Number 11 did not accomplish its goal of stopping the violence along the Missouri/Kansas border as guerrilla attacks on army installations continued until the end of the war in 1865. Mail and supply deliveries into the district required military escorts; otherwise, they would be attacked by Bushwhacker units. The Bushwhackers maintained their presence and were still considered to be in control of the Burnt District and used the area as a base from which to continue to attack and harass military units and transports.

An unintended consequence of the order, after the initial months, is that the jayhawking raids into the region stopped since there was nothing left for the Jayhawkers to steal. Throughout the rest of his life, General Ewing justified the act by maintaining that it did prevent another Kansas massacre on the scale of what occurred in Lawrence (Roe 6).

The wildly unpopular Ewing was removed as the Commander of the District of the West in January of 1864. His replacement quickly

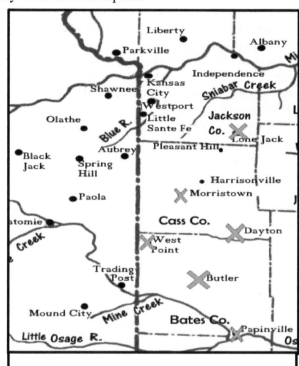

Figure 103: The "Burnt District" after execution of Order Number 11. The towns marked with an "X" were eliminated from the map. There were many other, smaller towns also eliminated by the order.

rescinded Order Number 11. Some residents of the Burnt District returned and tried to rebuild their lives. Many did not. In 1865, after the war was over, the *Olathe Mirror* made this comment about the Burnt District:

Scarcely anything marks the 'ancient habitations' of man except the long and blackened chimneys of former buildings, standing boldly out, the mournful representatives of devastating war; and nothing marks the former cultivation of the land, except here and there, but the remains of old fences, dismal fields of weeds and frightful reptiles (July 7, 1865)

After the war, Radical Unionists from Kansas City would launch an effort to repopulate the Burnt District with the "right kind of people". A massive marketing campaign was undertaken in northern states to attract citizens and immigrants from Union states to come and take over the already cleared fields and homesteads for pennies on the dollar. The Federal Government helped by publishing notices informing landowners in the Burnt District that they must return and pay all back taxes or forfeit their land. Many did not return making more land available. By 1870, the pre-war, southern leaning population of the Burnt District had been substantially replaced by new northern landowners. At this point only approximately 30% of the residents who had been evicted had returned to reclaim their land. This lack of local memory and knowledge of the Border War events had effectively removed the pain of Order Number 11 from the history of the area (Rafiner 261).

What Happened To. . .

Olathe

Olathe, which had been declining in population since the start of the war because of the danger of its location near the Missouri border, was devastated by Quantrill's Raid. Many families gathered up their belongings and moved to Leavenworth to be closer to the Federal Army post, or further west to get away from the danger on the border. Businesses, most of them decimated by the looting during the raid, were mostly closed and commerce was nonexistent. Business owners, many of whom had just lost everything to the guerrillas, were not willing to replenish their stock and take the risk of losing it again in another raid. Most of the buildings, homes and businesses stood empty.

Property owners were not charging rent, rather, they were looking for anyone they could pay to stay in Olathe and live in their buildings to protect them. Property could not be sold as no buyers were willing to buy in such a dangerous location. The Federal Army sent two companies of the 12th Regiment to Olathe to help protect the town, but at this point, there was not much to protect.

Olathe Population

Year	Population
1860	520
1861	260
1865	500
1870	1817
1880	2285
1900	3451
2020	142,000

Figure 104: Olathe Population from 1860-2020

The population chart shows that the population of the city was already dwindling prior to Quantrill's raid in September of 1862. Only half of residents who lived in Olathe in 1860 remained in 1861. The population increased back to pre-war numbers by 1865. This fact is a bit misleading because the number of residents in 1865 only included fifteen residents whose names were present on the 1860 census. A significant portion of the "new residents" in 1865 were comprised of squatters, Indians and freed slaves.

That said, Olathe never succumbed to the fate of many other Civil War-era small Kansas towns such as Lanesfield, Aubry, Squiresville and Quindaro, which had ceased to exist shortly after the war ended. One thing in Olathe's favor was the fact that it was still the county seat of Johnson County. This meant that even though much of the commerce in the city had ceased during the war years, the business of the county government continued, and thus traffic in and out of town continued.

One of the two town newspapers, the *Olathe Mirror*, destroyed during the Quantrill Raid, began printing again in the spring of 1863. During the war years, the paper only did enough printing to meet the needs of the county government by publishing legal notices. The publishers of the *Olathe Mirror* had this to say about their enterprise on July 11, 1863:

We have been asked why we don't revive the "Mirror" in full. During the past two years, we have been promised protection by our governors, generals and senators, notwithstanding the fact that every town in our county has been sacked from one to three times. Last spring, believing we would have the protection so long sought, we made arrangements to renew our paper in its old shape. But the protection we anticipated did not come and we have come to the conclusion not to start out anew until we can see fair indication of the end of our troubles. (Blair 1915 207)

The quote from the editors of the *Olathe Mirror* show the local dissatisfaction with the protection provided by the federal troops, a common feeling among most Kansas border residents at the time. Nothing would be done to try and provide more security for Kansas citizens until Quantrill returned to Kansas for the Lawrence Raid, which occurred a little over a month after the previous quote from the *Olathe Mirror* was printed. After the Lawrence Raid on August 21st, 1863, the bloody war on the Missouri/Kansas Border began to get significant national attention. This attention increased the pressure on the military commanders in Kansas to do a better job of protecting the citizens from the guerilla bands led by men such as Quantrill.

Olathe would recover. Historic property records show that many of the town founders, who abandoned their property during the war years, would come back once the war was over to rebuild and restart their lives in the city. The Sante Fe and California Trails would continue to be heavily used by wagon traffic up until around 1880, at which time, they would begin to be replaced by railroads, which also had a large presence in Olathe, giving the city further fuel for growth. Today, Olathe is currently the fourth largest city in Kansas, remains the county seat of Johnson County and continues to grow at a steady rate with a population in 2020 of 142,000.

James Lane

Jim Lane, the Liberator of Kansas, or the Grim Chieftain, was the William Quantrill on the Union side of the Border War. The primary difference was that Lane was a sitting U.S. Senator and an officer in the Union Army. Remember the quote about the victors writing history. In most stories about the two men, a reader could easily switch one name out for the other and the facts would still be true. Quantrill destroyed Lawrence; Lane destroyed Osceola and much of western Missouri. Quantrill burned and robbed the property of Union Sympathizers; Lane burned and robbed the property of Southern Sympathizers, etc.

Lane was able, due to his official capacity, to roam the countryside of Kansas and Missouri and do whatever struck his fancy at the time. Most of the time he and his "soldiers" acted like guerillas,

Figure 105: Senator/General James Lane. Image courtesy of the Library of Congress

but they did it under the flag of the United States Army, which to many people outside of Missouri, legitimatized his actions. Missouri residents, regardless of their political views, saw Lane and his men as criminals who murdered, robbed and devastated the Missouri landscape.

Lane would continue his military service through the end of the Civil War. In Kansas, like Quantrill in Missouri, Lane was a hero and extremely popular. In 1865, Lane was re-elected to the U.S. Senate, where early in his second term, he made some political mistakes that began to erode his popularity among his constituents. One such mistake was his practice of making promises to constituents if they would agree to back him in the election. During the election for his second term, he promised seventeen different men the position of "Marshalship of the District of Kansas". Obviously, he could not keep all of those promises and after the election, word began to get out as to what he had done. He "fixed" this problem by calling all seventeen men together and informed them:

> *Gentlemen, I was in a tight spot last winter when I promised each of you the marshalship for the District of Kansas. I am in a tighter spot today. What I did last winter, I did with the purest of motives. I wished for re-election not simply for my own personal good, but for the good of the State of Kansas. . . . I thought Kansas needed me in the Senate, and for that reason, I made promises which I cannot now fill. If I have deceived you, gentlemen, I believe that heaven will forgive me. But your [sic], who should have voted for me from the purest and highest impulses, were impelled only by sordid motives. You sold your votes, and I do not think any of you worthy in the sight of heaven to hold an office. I renounce you all, and in the interest of the State of Kansas, I will select an entirely new man. Good evening, gentlemen." (Bailes 203, citing Capitol Commonwealth, 12/23/1888)*

Lane's political mistakes would prove to be his undoing. He backed the reconstruction policies of President Andrew Johnson, which were very unpopular to Union supporters as they were thought to be too favorable to the southern states. To many Northerners, the southern states needed to be punished after the war, not coddled. Lane, who was far from pro-southern, had this to say in a speech in the U.S. Senate about South Carolina men early in his second term:

> *I would like to live long enough to see every white man in South Carolina in hell, and the Negroes inheriting their territory. It would not wound my feelings any day to find the dead bodies of rebel sympathizers pierced with bullet holes in every street and alley of Washington. Yes, I would regret this, for I would not like to witness all this waste of powder and lead. I would rather have them hung,*

and the ropes saved! Let them dangle until their stinking bodies rot and fall to the ground piece by piece. (Edmonds 242)

As is evidenced by the above quote, Lane's backing of Johnson's softer reconstruction policies was not due to his belief in those policies, but rather, can be attributed to a deal he made with President Johnson where he agreed to vote to uphold Johnson's veto of the Civil Rights Bill in April of 1866. This was a very popular bill with Lane's Party, the Radical Republicans, and opposing it would be costly from a political standpoint in the state of Kansas. To his credit, Lane stood by his word knowing that it could destroy him politically, which is exactly what happened (Bailes 204).

As has been mentioned earlier in this work, Lane was always known to be a "little bit crazy". This loss of backing from his supporters and other "Radical Republicans", hit him hard. It is said that Lane was very depressed and likely a little deranged by the middle of 1866. In the early summer of that year, Lane had been confined to his hotel room in St. Louis and was under suicide watch, due to repeated attempts to take his own life. He arrived back in Kansas in late June 1866.

On July 1, 1866, Lane had ventured out for a carriage ride with his brother in law, Mr. McCall. At one point the carriage stopped and Mr. McCall got out on one side and Lane got out on the other side. As he was exiting the carriage, Lane pulled a small pistol from his coat and said, "Goodbye Mac," and shot himself in the head. The *Atchison Daily Champion* says that "this fatal act was undoubtedly the result of a temporary mental aberration". They go on to report that Lane is the third member of his family to have "thus destroyed himself". James Lane would die ten days later from the self-inflicted wound on, July 11, 1866, near Leavenworth Kansas. He is buried in Oak Hill Cemetery, in Lawrence, Kansas.

The Atchison *Daily Champion* would sum up Lane's contribution to Kansas in this article:

His melancholy death will make a void in the State of Kansas that cannot be soon filled. The loss of no hundred men in the State would produce such a change in our political affairs as that of this bold, active, energetic partisan. No other man combines so many elements of popularity as did he. The amplitude and fertility of his resources; his rare talent for political leadership, for administration, and for controversy; his dauntless resolution; and his enthusiastic zeal in achieving a result – these are qualities which were peculiarly his, and we shall look for them in any other one man in vain. (2)

Missourians who had lived through the Border War likely had a different opinion of James Henry Lane.

Figure 106: James Henry Lane death photo. July 1866.
Image courtesy of www.canteymyerscollections.com

Charles "Doc" Jennison

If you recall Doc Jennison's status when we left him before the Olathe Raid, he had resigned his commission in April 1862, with the Union Army and in doing so, had made some very inflammatory speeches to his men before he left the army. In his speeches, he encouraged his men to resign and ride with him in "defense of Kansas".

These speeches did not sit well with federal commanders and they ordered Jennison arrested and held in a St. Louis jail.

While he was arrested and jailed, he would never be brought to trial as his incarceration was a significant public relations problem for the Union. His popularity in Kansas and the northern states put the Union Army in a tough spot. The army leadership just wanted Jennison to go away and stay out of the national spotlight. With this end in mind, he was quietly released from prison and sent back to Kansas where he lived as a civilian for about a year and a half. Then the raid on Lawrence happened.

Figure 107: Charles "Doc" Jennison

After the events in Lawrence, authorities decided that someone of Jennison's skills was needed to help enforce Order Number 11. Jennison, along with his newly formed 15th Kansas Cavalry, would terrorize Missourians for the remainder of the war. These men rode with Jennison's motto that "Missourians were alike – all disloyal" (Goodrich, Black Flag 134). To Jennison, it didn't matter which side of the war they favored, they were Missourians and thus needed to be punished. Jennison and his men would relish their role as the enforcers of Order Number 11 in the Burnt District.

Figure 109: Confederate General Sterling Price. Image courtesy of the Library of Congress

In the fall of 1864, Jennison's command would get its' first taste of action as they would be called upon to help defend Kansas and Missouri from General Sterling Price and his troops. The Rebels were making their way across Missouri to commandeer supplies and recruits from the Missourians who were loyal to the Southern cause. Jennison's 15th would take part in the Battle of Big Blue and the Battle of Westport. Lieutenant Colonel Jennison would be named by Major General Samuel R. Curtis to his "Role of Honor" for his valor at the Battle of Westport.

After Westport, Price would take his army and head for safer territory in Arkansas. Jennison's 15th Cavalry, under the command of Major General Alfred Pleasonton, caught up to the rebel force at Newtonia, Missouri. The two armies clashed at Newtonia but come nightfall, after Union reinforcements had arrived, General Price continued his retreat into Arkansas. The Union Army did not pursue them into Arkansas.

Figure 108: Site of the Battle of Newtonia

On the way home, Jennison and his men fell back into their old ways and jayhawked their way home through Missouri. Jennison was a true abolitionist and all of his actions displayed the fact that he felt slavery was wrong. In addition to robbing and burning the homes of Missourians in his travels, he also spared no opportunity to free slaves and attempted to get them into Kansas where they could be free. In December of 1864, an investigation would be opened by Major General James Blunt, into the behavior of Jennison and his men on their way back to Kansas after the Battle of Newtonia.

I have learned unofficially that the command under Col. C. R. Jennison, Fifteenth Kansas Volunteers, on their return from the Arkansas River, after the abandonment of the pursuit of Price, committed many acts of vandalism on their march through Washington and Benton Counties, Ark. This outrageous conduct of Colonel Jennison and a portion of his command (for if what I have heard is true it can be characterized in no other terms) was wholly unauthorized by superior officers and is very much deprecated. . . . I am causing an investigation into the conduct of Colonel Jennison in Northwestern Arkansas, with a view of meting out just punishment to the guilty parties. (Titterington)

One of the witnesses to Jennison's actions was Missouri Captain Green C. Stotts who had this to say in his statement:

Jennison has just passed through this vicinity on his return from Arkansas River. The night of the [November] 19th he stayed at Newtonia, the 20th at Sarcoxie, and the 21st at Dry Fork. Where he passed, the people are almost ruined, as their houses were robbed of the beds and bedding in many cases every blanket and quilt were taken; also, their clothing and every valuable that could be found, or the citizens forced to discover. All the horses, stock, cattle, sheep, oxen, and wagons were driven off. . .. Many of them have once sympathized with the rebellion, but nearly all of them have been quiet and cultivated their farms during last year, expecting the protection of U. S. troops. . .. There are cases where the men tore the clothing off of women in search of money and threatened to burn houses in order to get money is the common practice. They acted worse than guerrillas. (Titterington)

Jennison justified his actions by saying that he had been ordered by Union authorities to "desolate the country from the Arkansas River to Fort Scott and burn every house on the route." On June 23, 1865, Charles Jennison was dishonorably discharged from the service of the United States Army.

After his removal from the Union Army, Jennison moved to Leavenworth and went back to civilian life. He would serve on the Leavenworth City Council, be elected to the Kansas State Senate in 1865, and then re-elected in 1867. Despite being elected twice, it appears, based on newspaper articles of the time, that Jennison was not a popular man in Leavenworth. He was also known to own and operate several illegal gambling houses across western Kansas.

In 1871, he tried to get a pardon from President Grant for his wartime activities, the *Leavenworth Times* has this to say:

Application was made at the time for a pardon. Grant refused to recommend it, and Jennison has cursed Grant from that day to this. Jennison openly denounced Grant . . .. We do not believe the gambler [Jennison] has any such power over Pomeroy and Caldwell, and we trust the President will not permit any influence to move him to pardon a man who ten years has been, and now is a professed gambler, personally interested in a gambling hell in this city. (December 14, 1871)

Unlike many of his fellow Border War participants, Jennison would go on to live a relatively normal life after the Civil War ended. Charles "Doc" Jennison died in Leavenworth, Kansas, on June 21, 1884, at the age of fifty, of chronic respiratory disease. The *Kansas Prohibitionist* summed up Doc Jennison this way in his obituary in 1884, "The name of Charles R. Jennison will go down to remote generations with the history of Kansas, alike in glory and in shame."

Figure 110: Charles Jennison, later in life. Image taken between 1870 and 1880

George Todd and Bloody Bill Anderson

After the raid on Lawrence, during which Quantrill and his men burned a quarter of the town and killed at least 150 male citizens, Captain Quantrill took his men and went to Texas for the winter of 1863-1864. The raid on Lawrence had garnered a great deal of negative national attention and even forced the Confederate Government to "officially" withdraw their support of Quantrill and his Bushwhackers. Unofficially, the Confederate Government still relished the work done by the Bushwhackers, and through unofficial channels, encouraged them to continue with that work. On their way to Texas for the winter, Quantrill's men attacked Fort Blair, in Baxter Springs, Kansas. While failing to take the small fort after a full-frontal assault, Quantrill's men unexpectantly ran into a Union supply caravan coming into town. It was in the ambush of this wagon train that they killed at least one hundred Union troops and carried off a significant amount of supplies. This action, when coupled with the atrocities from the Lawrence Raid, was difficult, even for Southern Sympathizers, to justify as being part of the war effort. The guerrillas continued to embarrass the Confederacy in Texas when they lynched a judge, a sheriff and another man in Tyler, Texas, in retaliation for a gunfight with a Texas posse.

Quantrill began to lose control of the men in the winter of 1863, which might explain some of these actions, as the military leadership started to erode within Quantrill's command. Late in the winter of 1863, Quantrill's command was fractured. Bloody Bill Anderson made the decision, in an angry rage over the disciplining of one of his men, to leave Quantrill's unit and take some men with him. When the men headed back to Missouri in March of 1864, they would be comprised of two individual units; one led by Quantrill and the other by Anderson.

William "Bloody Bill" Anderson's personality and hatred of Union soldiers are said to have taken a dark turn earlier in the year when before the Lawrence raid, his three younger sisters, Josephine 14, Mary 16, and Jennie 10, were arrested by federal forces due to their relation to Anderson. As has been previously mentioned, the prison in which they were being held collapsed on August 13, 1863. Anderson's 14-year-old sister, Josephine was killed and his other sisters, Jennie and Mary, were seriously injured during the collapse. According to reports, this event sent Anderson off the deep end and it was at this stage in his guerrilla career that he truly started to earn his name, "Bloody Bill".

Once back in Missouri the two units, along with other guerrilla outfits, would pick up where they left off raiding Union troops, disrupting mail and supply deliveries. They would also add hijacking riverboats to their repertoire. The Bushwhackers would pick an advantageous point in the river and then simply start firing on the passing riverboats until the boat's captain agreed to pull over so the goods and men on the boat could be dealt with. Union leadership eventually mandated

Figure 111: Bloody Bill Anderson

that all riverboats would put up metal sheets on the pilothouse so the boats could make it through the gauntlet that was the Missouri River. While this tactic was effective, the problem soon became that riverboat companies could find no captains willing to pilot the boats, due to the danger presented on the trip. The *Kansas City Journal* wrote this about the condition of the border counties in the early summer of 1864:

> *What is the condition of the truly loyal people of the border counties of Missouri south of the river? Simply, one of siege. Outside the military posts and their immediate vicinity, no man of known and open loyalty can safely live for a moment. The loyal people are collected in the scattered towns and military posts, while to all practical intents and purposes the rebels hold the possession of the country (June 14, 1864).*

In late June, Quantrill, injured from a previous skirmish, decided to take a break. He would take his wife/mistress, Kate King, and a few trusted men and go to Howard County, which is located just northwest of Columbia. His plan was to lay low and recuperate until later in the summer when General Sterling Price brought his Confederate Army into Missouri. At which point he would rejoin the fray. When Quantrill informed his Lieutenant George Todd of his plan, Todd was furious, calling Quantrill a coward.

A few days later Todd and Quantrill argued again, this time reportedly over a dispute in a card game. Whatever the reason, it appears that when Quantrill left for Howard County, Todd took command of the majority of Quantrill's men. Several of the men left when Todd took over. He was not particularly respected as a leader and had the reputation for being reckless with little concern for the lives of his men. He was known as a fierce warrior and, for that reason, many of the men who shared this trait would stay with him and continue to wreak havoc on the border.

Figure 112: George Todd, date unknown. Image courtesy of www.Canteymyerscollection.com

Without Quantrill's calming effect on the men, Todd and Anderson would increase the ferocity of the attacks on anyone, both north and south of the Missouri River, who was thought to support the Union. They would attack Union troops and kill all the soldiers forcing them to strip to their underwear before being executed. It was very common in the summer of 1864, and even for years after the war, for travelers to find rotting, naked corpses or skeletons throughout the Missouri countryside (Brownlee 196).

Bill Anderson would expand his actions to the east into Lafayette and Saline Counties. Anderson would begin writing letters to newspapers, military commanders and other important Union leaders. The letters were quite eloquent and disproved the notion Anderson was a bloodthirsty, illiterate devil. The letters would ask for the release of certain prisoners or to clarify facts that had been printed about a certain skirmish or engagement. Most of the letters contained mention of the men that he had killed or threats to kill more men depending on the action of the recipient.

One note that was not written by Anderson but was attributed to him was pinned to a Union cavalryman who was killed and scalped in central Missouri in late July. The note read, "You come to hunt bushwhackers. Now you are skelpt [scalped]. Clemyent [Archie Clement] skept [scalped] you, Wm. Anderson." (Brownlee 205) This note, whose spelling and grammar tell us that Anderson did not write it, brings up another point regarding Anderson. One of the traits often attributed to Anderson that adds depth to the "Bloody Bill" nickname is the fact that he or his men would often scalp his victims. This is a fact. It is also a fact that this was a fairly common practice among Bushwhackers, Jayhawker and Union soldiers throughout the Border War. It is possible that Bloody Bill and his men did this more than others, but there is no factual basis for that assumption. This is another situation where a heinous act from men on the losing side is highlighted and amplified while the same act is ignored for those on the winning side.

In the late summer of 1864, word came from General Price that he was finally preparing for his campaign into Missouri. The three leaders, Quantrill, Todd and Anderson, were asked to move their operations north of the Missouri River to force the Union Army in St. Louis to expend men and resources to deal with the guerrillas north of the river. During this time, the three leaders would work together to accomplish certain missions. Acrimony and disagreement between the three would make these joint efforts few and far between. The three leaders did meet with Price in October and were each given orders to further disrupt northern Missouri, paying particular attention to railroad infrastructure in that region. All three men left with those orders and would succeed in their mission to a certain extent. It is clear from their actions after the meeting that they would work to accomplish the orders if, and only if, it fit within their own plans.

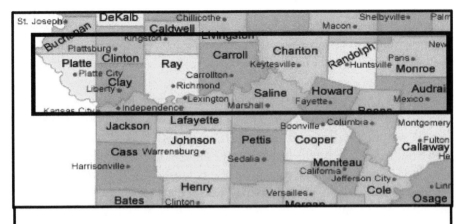

Figure 113: Enclosed area shows the focus region for the Bushwhackers in late summer/early fall of 1864.

It was with disruption of rail lines in mind that Anderson and his men came to Centralia, Missouri on September 27, 1864. In downtown Centralia, wearing stolen Union uniforms, they stopped a train carrying 125 passengers, 24 of which were Union soldiers returning home after participating in Sherman's March in Georgia. After dividing the civilians from the soldiers, Anderson lined up the soldiers and asked for a volunteer officer to step forward. Sergeant Thomas Goodman step-ped forward, thinking that he would be sacrificing himself but saving the lives of the rest of the soldiers. He was incorrect.

Rather than shooting Goodman, Anderson and his men commenced shooting the other 23 soldiers. All the soldiers were

Figure 114: Centralia, Missouri, the massacre occurred in town while the battle took place just east of town.

shot, their bodies mutilated, some being scalped. The guerrillas then set fire to the train and the station and left town. Sergeant Goodman was taken prisoner in hopes of a prisoner exchange. He would escape from the rebels several days later. The Centralia Massacre was only the first action on that day as the Battle of Centralia would occur later that afternoon. That battle did not go well for the Union forces either.

Around 3:00 pm that afternoon, Major Andrew Vern Johnston, a former schoolteacher with little military experience, leading 146 men who comprised the newly formed, and largely untrained, 39th Missouri Mounted Regiment, arrived in a field east of Centralia to make Anderson and his Bushwhackers pay for their deeds in town, earlier that day. Anderson had over 300 men, two-thirds of which were waiting in a tree line, ready for a second charge if needed. Seeing only about 80 men, Johnston challenged Anderson to stand and fight. Instead, Anderson's 80 men charged the Union skirmish line on horseback. The rebels wiped out the Union forces in about three minutes. When it was all over, 123 of the 147 Union troops were dead. Only three confederates were killed in the battle, the other 200 men waiting in the tree line never even got into the battle, as they were not needed. Frank James would later say that it was his brother, Jesse, who fired the shot that killed Major Johnston on that day.

Figure 115: Wanted Poster for "Bloody Bill". Circulated after the Centralia Massacre.

By October of 1864, Todd and his men were riding with General Jo Shelby and his cavalry unit. With Shelby, Todd's men would be involved in several skirmishes in front of Price's army as it moved west across Missouri. Todd would be killed at the age of 25 while fighting with Shelby at the Second Battle of Independence on October 21st. Shelby's men had pushed the Kansas Militia out of Independence after intense block to block fighting (Brownlee 226). Approximately two and a half miles out of town, Todd was struck in the neck by a sniper's bullet, knocking him from his horse. George W. Todd is buried at Woodlawn Cemetery in Independence, Missouri.

Figure 116: George Todd's grave, Woodlawn Cemetery, Independence,

One week after Todd's death in Independence, Anderson and his men would be involved in the Battle of Albany, which took place just north of Orrick, Missouri, in Ray County on October 27, 1864. The Bushwhackers were resting in camp when a small unit of federal

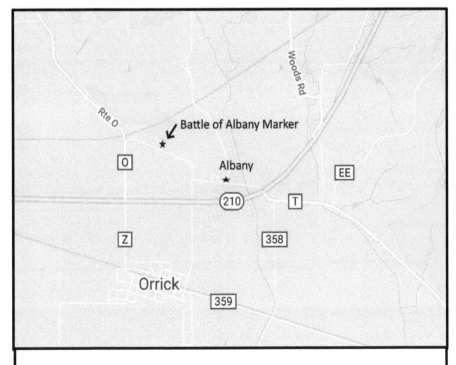

Figure 117: Location of the Battle of Albany, Ray County, Missouri

soldiers attacked. Thinking he had the advantage, Anderson and about twenty of his men, mounted their horses and chased the Union soldiers as they ran away from the battle. What Anderson did not know, was that over 300 men from Fifty-first and Thirty-third Missouri Militia had set a trap and were waiting in the tree line for the Bushwhackers. The Union troops opened fire as Anderson and his men approached their position. Eight of Anderson's men were killed with the first volley. Captain Anderson and two other men made it through the Union line and would have escaped if they had just kept riding. Instead, Anderson saw one of his men go down and went back to rescue him. This valiant act would cost both men their lives.

Found on his body were a picture of Anderson and his wife, some letters from his wife, a lock of her hair, a small confederate flag and orders from Major General Price. The orders read as follows:

Captain Anderson with his command, will at once proceed to the north side of the Missouri River and permanently destroy the North Missouri Railroad, going as far east as practicable. He will report his operations at least every two days. By order of Major-General Price.

Bloody Bill's body was taken to Richmond where it was dragged through the streets in celebration of the death of the notorious Guerrilla. William "Bloody Bill" Anderson is buried in the southwest corner of the

Figure 118: William Anderson gravesite, located in the southwest corner of the Mormon Cemetery in Richmond, Missouri

Mormon Cemetery in Richmond, Missouri. The *Lawrence Tribune* reported Anderson's death in this manner:

From the St. Jo. Herald, we copy the following account of the killing of the Missouri butcher, Bill Anderson. Kansas again has reason to

be thankful. ---Todd is gone; Anderson is gone; may Quantrill soon follow. (November 3, 1864)

Figure 119: Bloody Bill Anderson's Death Photo. Taken in Richmond, Missouri, on October 27, 1864.

When General Price's raid into Missouri proved unsuccessful, he and his army were driven out of the state by General Blunt in the fall of 1864. Price's failure led Quantrill to decide it was time to leave Missouri. With this journey in mind, he put out the call for his men to gather in Lafayette County. From there, they would start the trek out of Missouri to the east. It is a common belief that he planned to go to Virginia where he felt that General Lee was very close to surrendering his troops to General Grant. Quantrill's plan was for he and his men to mix in with General Lee's troops and thus be granted a pardon like any other surrendering Confederate soldier. It was important to get the official pardon because, in Missouri, his men were considered "outlaws", rather than soldiers. Quantrill feared that if they surrendered in Missouri they would be arrested as criminals and sent to prison or executed, rather than be pardoned.

Figure 120: Jesse and Frank James, 1872. Image courtesy of the U.S. Army Corps of Engineers

In response to his call, only 33 men showed up in Lafayette County to ride with Quantrill. This was quite a difference for a commander who at one time commanded armies of three to four hundred men. Frank James and 17-year-old, Jesse James were part of this small group that headed to the east in December of 1864. This would be Jesse's only time to ride with Quantrill. The future, famous outlaw and his older brother Frank had been riding with various guerrilla leaders during the summer of 1864, including participating in the Centralia Massacre with Bloody Bill Anderson.

Quantrill's plan was to ride to the southeast into Tennessee where they could more easily make their way east to eventually meet up with Lee's Army of Virginia. The group would live off the land robbing farms and small settlements along the way to support their travel needs. The plan called for the group to avoid attracting any federal attention, as their primary goal was to get out of Missouri.

In mid-December, early on their way out of the state, they rode into Tuscumbia, Missouri, a small federal post about thirty miles southwest of Jefferson City. Donning federal uniforms and, Quantrill calling himself Captain William Clarke, leader of the 4th Missouri Cavalry, he asked to see the post commander. While sit-ting with the post commander in his private office, Quantrill pulled out a pistol and forced the commander to surrender all of his troops.

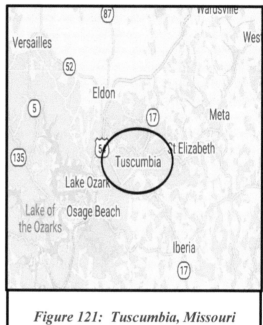

Figure 121: Tuscumbia, Missouri

The guerrillas then commenced loading anything of value, blankets, coats, food, guns and ammunition into wagons to be taken with them on their journey east, forcing the surrendered federal troops to assist them in getting across the Osage River, by operating the pulley system which powered the ferry. After reaching the opposite bank of the river, they quickly dumped the extra guns and ammunition into the river, sank the ferry and continued on their way. All of this happened without a single shot being fired.

In the northwest corner of Arkansas, near Pocahontas, a handful of men decided to leave the group and head to Texas, intending to find another group, either regular army or guerrilla band, with whom they would continue to fight for the Confederacy. Jesse James was one of those who decided to leave at this time, his brother Frank stayed with Quantrill. Crossing into Tennessee, Quantrill's group would gradually work their way north into southern Kentucky, which like Missouri, had many residents who were sympathetic to the Southern cause. The smaller size of the group, now under 30 men, made it easier to travel and attract less attention.

Arriving in Hartford, Kentucky, on January 22, 1864, the men rode directly to the Union camp where, acting as a Union captain, Quantrill

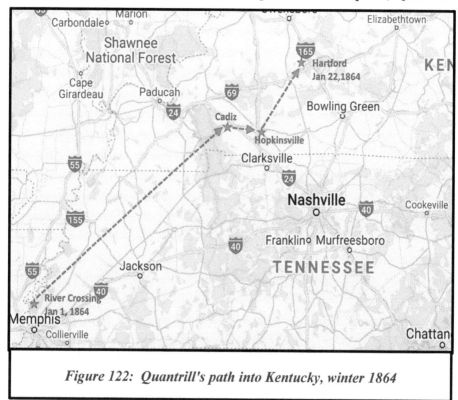

Figure 122: Quantrill's path into Kentucky, winter 1864

asked the post commander to provide a guide to take the men to the Ohio River. Colonel Q.C. Shanks, the post commander, saw no reason to doubt Quantrill, he would later say, "Their uniforms and good behavior whilst in this place and the conversation we had with said 'Clark' sufficiently satisfied us that he and his company were federal" (Leslie 346). After accepting the men as federal soldiers, Shanks readily provided Quantrill with a guide. Two other soldiers, looking for safe passage into the area, would join Quantrill's men with the guide and leave Hartford with the imposters. None of the three men who joined the group would live to see the end of the trip. The body of the guide, Lieutenant Barnett, would be found with a bullet through his head, sixteen miles from Hartford. He had served his purpose. The other two soldiers' bodies were found along the trail.

Throughout the rest of the winter and early spring of 1864, Quantrill and his men would return to their old ways, bushwhacking in Kentucky rather than in Kansas and Missouri. In their new home, they would regularly pair up with Kentucky guerrillas to create havoc for the federal troops in whatever way they could. At one point they joined forces with noted guerrilla fighter, Sue Mundy, incorrectly known as the "Girl Guerrilla".

It is now widely believed that Sue Mundy was actually Marcellus Jerome Clark a young, baby-faced guerilla leader in Kentucky, who, in the Spring of 1864 had become the most feared guerilla leader in north central Kentucky (Leslie 347). Sue Mundy is first mentioned in the *Louisville Journal* on October 11, 1864, where editor George D. Prentice describes "her" this way, "[Munday] dresses in male attire,

Figure 123: Sue Mundy, aka the Girl Guerrilla, aka Marcellus Jerome Clark

generally sporting a full confederate uniform. She is possessed of a comely form, is a bold rider and a dashing leader." (it is only in this first mention that the name is spelled "Munday", from then on, it is spelled "Mundy".

The "girl guerilla" story would reach national acclaim after it was printed in the *Louisville Journal*. Editor Prentice was using this story as a means to criticize the current Department of Kentucky leader Major Steven G. Burbridge, the Federal Commander in Kentucky, with whom he strongly disagreed and attacked regularly using his platform as editor of the paper. There is controversy over the "girl guerilla" story in that some sources say that Sue Mundy was simply a character that Prentice made up to embarrass Burbridge, as if he was saying, "Burbridge is so incompetent that he has been bested by a young girl." Most historians now believe that Sue Mundy existed but was, in fact, a man named Marcellus Jerome Clark. Jerome Clark was captured after a skirmish and taken to Louisville for trial on March 13th, where he was found guilty and hung on March 15, 1864. His last words were:

> *I am a regular Confederate soldier and have served in the Confederate Army four years, I have taken many federal soldiers prisoner and have always treated them kindly . . .. I hope in and die for the Confederate cause" (Leslie 361).*

Clarke's execution occurred after a significant shift in federal strategy for dealing with guerillas in Kentucky, when in February of 1864, General John M. Palmer was named head of the Department of Kentucky. Palmer was a staunch abolitionist and Radical Republican who believed he had a plan that would resolve the problems presented by the guerillas in his territory. Palmer planned to use informants and bounty hunters to catch guerillas. With that in mind, on April 1st, Palmer hired 19-year-old Edwin Terrill (often spelled Terrell) and his thirty men as part of his new "secret service".

Figure 124: General John M. Palmer, Department of Kentucky

"Captain" Terrill was far from an upstanding citizen. As early as January of that same year, Terrill and his men, dressed in Confederate uniforms and pretending to be part of the "Sue Mundy" command, had terrorized Nelson County. In the small town of Bloomfield, Terrill and his Confederate imposters were going about their business of robbing stores and citizens while the real Sue Mundy gang, led by Jerome Clark, rode in and chased the Terrill command out of the town to the cheers of the residents. Four months later this "upstanding citizen" was hired by the Federal Government to infiltrate and apprehend the guerilla groups that were operating in Kentucky. His primary mission was to capture William Quantrill.

The war was not going well for the Confederate Army. On March 29, General Lee had surrendered the city of Petersburg, Virginia and by April 2nd, the Confederate Government was forced to evacuate the Confederate Capital of Richmond. Seven days later on April 9th, Lee surrendered to General Grant at Appomattox Courthouse, which meant that Quantrill's plan to surrender with Lee in Virginia was not going to happen. John McCorkle tells us that Quantrill's new plan was to surrender in Louisville (Peterson 404).

On the morning of May 10th, Terrill and Quantrill would cross paths at the James H. Wakefield farm, five miles south of Taylorsville, Kentucky. Quantrill and his men, on their way to Louisville, possibly to surrender, had stopped at the farm previously and had become friendly with the southern sympathizing farmer, James Wakefield. On this morning, as Quantrill's band of twenty-one men rode into the farmstead, a heavy rain began to fall,

Figure 125: Captain Edwin Terrill. The name is often spelled "Terrell", but I have been unable to find evidence in historical records to confirm which spelling is correct.

which forced the men into the barn to get out of the rain. Terrill and his guerilla hunters, who had seen the tracks of this large group of men as they rode north on the Bloomfield-Taylorsville Road, ambushed Quantrill's men while they were comfortably waiting out the rain in the barn. Most of Quantrill's men made it to their horses and rode quickly away, but several of the horses broke loose in the confusion which forced several other men to run and dive into a pond where they lay low until the pursuers went past at which point, they scurried into woods.

Quantrill himself was not so lucky. His horse, a new mount, bucked and would not allow Quantrill to get into the saddle. Giving up, he started to run with the other men. Hearing his call for help, one of his men came back and tried to help Quantrill get up behind him on his horse. While trying to get up behind this man, the horse was shot in the hip and started running wildly. Giving up on that avenue of escape, he looked to another man who offered him a seat behind him on his mount, but as Quantrill tried to get up on the second horse, a bullet from one of Terrill's men struck him in the spine and paralyzed him from the waist

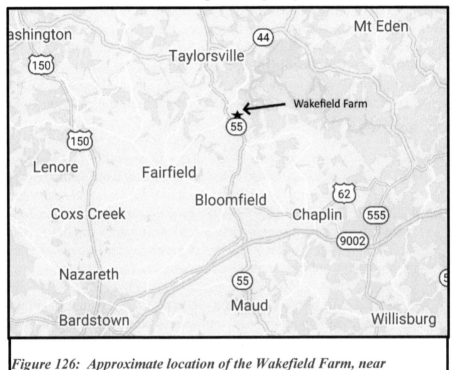

Figure 126: Approximate location of the Wakefield Farm, near Taylorsville, Kentucky

down. He fell facedown into a puddle of mud. The two men who had tried to help him, were both chased down and killed.

After the excitement died down, Terrill's men came back and found Quantrill lying in the mud. They searched his pockets and took anything of value in addition to stripping him of his boots and pistols. They then carried him into the Wakefield house, where their comrades were already looting the house. Questioned by Terrill, Quantrill maintained that he was Captain Clarke of the Fourth Missouri Confederate Cavalry. He asked Terrill if he could stay at the farm to die. Terrill eventually agreed to this request likely due to Quantrill's paralysis and the difficulty he would have transporting the prisoner to Louisville. He left Quantrill on the farm and went off to continue his work searching for William Quantrill (Leslie 365). Before leaving, he made Wakefield promise that he would not allow the prisoner to leave the farm promising that if he did, the entire farm would be burned to the ground.

Over the next two nights, several of Quantrill's men came back to the farm to see him and offer their services to take him someplace safe. Frank James, who had not been with the group at the farm suggested he be taken out into the woods of Kentucky where no Union troops would ever be able to find him. Quantrill refused the offer as he did not want his friend, John Wakefield, to pay the price for allowing him to leave. It is also likely that Quantrill knew that surviving in the woods while being paralyzed was not a realistic option. John Edwards recalls Quantrill's last words to his men as he asked them to leave him and take care of themselves:

I cannot live. I have run a long time; I have fought to kill, and I have killed; I regret nothing. The end is close at hand. I am resting easy here and will die so. You do not know how your devotion has touched my heart, nor can you ever understand how grateful I am for the love you have shown for me. Try to get back to your homes and avoid, if you can, the perils which beset you and may God bless you and yours. (437)

Captain Terrill and his guerrilla hunters finally figured out the identity of the man lying paralyzed on the Wakefield farm and on May 12th, a Conestoga wagon was sent to transport Quantrill to the military prison hospital in Louisville in as much comfort as possible. Along the way, Terrill would make sure that multiple doctors would treat Quantrill to ensure that he lived to be presented to General Palmer at his headquarters in Louisville. At least two female admirers also stopped the procession to give Quantrill flowers. Captain Terrill presented Quantrill to Palmer in Louisville around 11 am on May 13th. Terrill was paid for his accomplishment, then promptly fired from his job in the Secret Service and sent on his way. Terrill had accomplished his primary mission which was to capture Quantrill. With that goal accomplished, the federal authorities did not want to have to deal with Captain Terrill any longer.

The paralyzed Quantrill was taken to the prison hospital where he would spend the short remainder of his life. Inside the Kentucky Military command structure, there was significant doubt as to whether the man in the Louisville prison hospital was, in fact, William Clarke Quantrill. This likely explains why newspapers of the time did not loudly proclaim the capture of the nation's most notorious guerilla leader. Rumors abounded that he was in Texas with Confederate General Price and the person lying in the hospital bed was simply an imposter who took the infamous name.

William Clarke Quantrill, an upbeat and friendly patient in the Louisville Military Hospital, died from his wounds at 4 pm on June 6, 1864, a month after he arrived. He was only 27-years-old. His body was unceremoniously buried in an unmarked grave in Louisville's St. Mary's Catholic Cemetery, now known as St. John's Catholic Cemetery. Father Michael Power, the Catholic priest who had cared for Quantrill during his hospital stay and converted him to Catholicism during that time, ordered the unmarked grave. Father Power was reportedly following Quantrill's directions concerning his grave as Quantrill was concerned that if the public knew about the burial site, the grave would be desecrated. Quantrill had also asked that the kitchen staff scatter food waste on the grave to ensure that it did not look like a new grave.

The strange story of Quantrill's final resting place, which would go on for the next 120 years, was just beginning.

Quantrill's Bones

William Walter Scott, a boyhood friend of Quantrill, newspaper editor and writer, enters the scene around 1870. Around this time, Quantrill's mother, Caroline, was on a mission to find out what really happened to her eldest son. W.W. Scott and Mrs. Quantrill would become reacquainted and he would begin to assist in her attempt to learn more about her son's activities as well as ascertain the location of his physical remains. Scott had an ulterior motive in that he aspired to write a book about Quantrill and thus earn back much of what he was spending to help Mrs. Quantrill. Out of respect for Mrs. Quantrill, a woman that he truly seemed to care for, Scott had decided to research for the project, but not publish the book until Mrs. Quantrill had passed away. This was because the book would likely have had some negative things to say about Quantrill and Scott did not want to upset her. Scott seemed like a man whose heart was in the right place and over the next thirty years he would go to extreme lengths to try and help Mrs. Quantrill, even though she turned on him several times throughout their relationship.

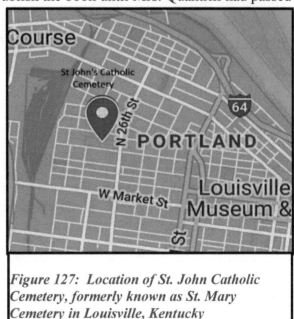

Figure 127: Location of St. John Catholic Cemetery, formerly known as St. Mary Cemetery in Louisville, Kentucky

Scott went on a scouting trip to Louisville in 1884, to attempt to locate Quantrill's grave in St. Mary Cemetery, now called St. John

Catholic Cemetery. Upon his return, Scott informed Mrs. Quantrill that he had spoken to the cemetery sexton and his wife and was able to confirm the exact location of Quantrill's unmarked grave. Fortunately the sexton was the same man, along with his wife, who held that position at the time of Quantrill's death twenty years earlier.

Mrs. Quantrill and Scott would return to Louisville in December 1887, to ask that the bones be allowed to be taken back to Dover for reburial. The sexton's wife, now the official sexton as her husband had passed away, would not allow this as she was fearful of rules regarding the moving of corpses. Instead, it was agreed that the bones would be dug up, placed in a zinc box and then reburied in the same location.

It was a cold and rainy December 7, 1887, when W.W. Scott stood in the rain and watched the unhappy gravedigger dig into the unmarked grave. Eventually, bones were found, many of which were brittle and crumbled to the touch. A skull was found, and Scott wrapped it in newspaper and hid it in his coat. The rest of the bones were put in a box, that was not lined with zinc, and buried just a few feet below the surface in the same spot. Mrs. Quantrill would identify the skull the next day as her son's by noting a chipped tooth that matched one that William had chipped as a young man. Mrs. Quantrill would not allow Scott to take the skull back to the sexton maintaining that skull should be buried in Dover with the remains of other family members. The pair left Louisville but the skull remained at their hotel, in a box, wrapped in newspaper.

Mrs. Quantrill would constantly badger Scott to go and get the rest of the bones and bring them back to Dover. She reportedly told him that she would deal with the sexton if he could get the bones. Scott did not want to lie to the sexton but eventually agreed to go back to Louisville and get the rest of the bones, under the pretense of wanting to put the skull in the box with the rest of Quantrill's bones. Scott was successful in digging up and taking the bones and the skull back to Dover with him. The plan was to bury them in the Dover Cemetery next to his brothers and father. The bones would "temporarily" be stored on the second floor of the Dover newspaper office which also served as Mr. Scott's residence. Mrs. Quantrill would later write to the sexton in Louisville and claim no knowledge of the deception, placing all blame on Scott for any trickery.

This accusation may have annoyed Scott in such a manner that he decided to try to sell the skull, still stored in a box in his office. In a letter dated December 17, 1887, to Major Franklin G. Andrews, secretary of the Kansas State Historical Society, Scott enclosed a lock of hair and asked what Quantrill's skull would be worth to the Historical Society. A tentative deal was struck, and Adams was going to try and raise $25 - $30 for the purchase. At this point, Scott backed out of the deal citing the fact that he was afraid Mrs. Quantrill would hear about the transaction. This failed transaction did not stop Scott from continuing to try to figure out a way to make some money from the bones in an effort to recoup his expenses (Kansas City Times, April 13, 1973).

Between 1887 and 1889, Mrs. Quantrill and Scott would travel through Kentucky and Missouri spending time with some of her son's friends and soldiers. Scott accompanied her on most of these trips, footing the expenses for both he and Mrs. Quantrill. On one such trip to Missouri, Scott stopped to meet again with the Kansas Historical Society, to again attempt to negotiate the sale of the skull to that group. This time he would sweeten the deal with two shin bones that he had removed from the box. Like the previous attempt, no sale was finalized, but for some unknown reason, the historical society would maintain possession of the shin bones.

It wasn't until the spring of 1889 that Mrs. Quantrill returned to Dover. She wanted the bones stored in Scott's office to be buried in the local cemetery. The community leaders of Dover were not thrilled about having someone with Quantrill's reputation buried in their local cemetery. Eventually, they agreed, with the condition that the service would be private, and no marker be placed on the grave. All parties agreed to this provision and less than six people attended the ceremony. It is unknown how many of Quantrill's bones made it into the grave in Dover. We know that Scott kept the skull and three arm bones. In addition, the two shin bones were still in the custody of the Kansas Historical Society.

Unfortunately, W.W. Scott, who had been loyal to Mrs. Quantrill for over thirty years, would never get to publish his book as he passed away before Mrs. Quantrill in November of 1902. After his death, his wife sent a letter to the Kansas State Historical Society asking them to keep private the fact that Scott had tried to sell the skull. She feared that this would besmirch his good name if this news become public. Scott's wife would eventually sell all her husband's papers, as well as Quantrill's three arm bones, to William E. Connelley, an officer of the Kansas Historical Society. You might recognize Connelley's name as the author who would write one of the first books about Quantrill entitled *Quantrill and Border Wars,* in 1910. Connelley, after trying, unsuccessfully, to trade the bones, for various other western relics, would eventually donate the bones to the Kansas Historical Society. Connelley's deal with the historical society stipulated that nothing regarding the purchase of the bones would become public until Mrs. Quantrill died.

Mrs. Quantrill, who was said to be a woman who would "eventually wear out her welcome in most places", bounced around in her old age, spending time at several "retirement homes" in addition to the county poorhouse. Before his death, Scott would secure a place for her in the Oddfellows Home for Women in Springfield, Ohio. She passed away at the Oddfellows Home on November 23, 1903. She was 83-years-old.

Only three days passed between her death and the announcement from the Kansas State Historical Society that they had acquired a lock of hair and three bones from William Quantrill and these would be put on public display. The public response to this announcement was harsh. Most newspapers and clergy denounced the public display and called on the Historical Society to reverse their decision to display the bones. The Reverend J.T. McFarland from Topeka's First Methodist Church had this to say:

> *The bones of a good man should be permitted to sleep unmolested; the bones of a wicked man should be left to rot with his memory. My motion is, and I would like to have a rising vote of the people of Kansas in its support, that the bones of William C. Quantrill, cattle thief, bandit and cutthroat, be thrown into the Kaw River and the space be preserved in our Historical Society rooms for mementoes of things honorable and of good repute. (Leslie 417)*

The Historical Society did not back down. The bones were publicly displayed until 1910. During this time, there were several "Quantrill Sightings" by people who felt that Quantrill was still alive and living in Canada. Tired of fighting this type of misinformation, the society pulled the bones and put them in their archeology lab, far from public display.

Quantrill's skull has had an even more interesting journey. Around 1910 someone in the Zeta Chapter of Alpha Phi fraternity received the skull from W. W. Scott's son, William. The skull was then used in fraternity rituals for the next thirty-two years. The fraternity folded in 1942 and the skull was purchased by an Alpha Phi member for sentimental reasons. The skull was given to the Dover Historical Society in 1972. A wax mold of the skull was made and kept in the refrigerator at the Dover Historical Society headquarters. The actual skull was displayed under a glass case in their museum.

Fast forward almost 80 years and the box of bones is still in a dark location with the Kansas Historical Society and the skull is still in the Reeves Museum in Dover, Ohio. Enter Robert L. Hawkins III, an attorney, Civil War enthusiast and Commander in Chief of the Missouri Division of the Sons of Confederate Veterans. Hawkins would make it his mission over the next five years, to provide a dignified burial for the remaining bones of William Quantrill.

After much negotiation between the Kansas Historical Society, the Missouri Department of Natural Resources and the city of Dover, Ohio, it was agreed that the bones still in the possession of the Kansas Historical Society, would be buried at the Confederate Cemetery in Higginsville, Missouri.

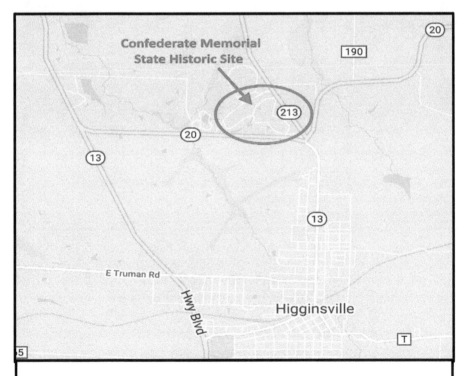

Figure 128: Confederate Memorial State Historic Site, Higginsville, Missouri, location of one of Quantrill's gravesites

Figure 129: Quantrill's grave located at the Confederate Memorial State Historic Site in Higginsville, Missouri

The Cemetery is located on the site of the Confederate Veterans' Home, where several of the men who rode with Quantrill passed their final days and where their remains are buried. Justifying the moving of the bones to the Confederate Cemetery, Hawkins stated:

We do not wish him buried where people are ashamed of him. It is not our intention to unreasonably glorify him. We are recognizing not just Quantrill but the Partisan Rangers who rode into the brush with him, forced there by occupation authorities" (Springfield News- Leader, Oct 25, 1992).

On October 24, 1992, six hundred people would attend the funeral of William Quantrill in Higginsville, Missouri. The coffin, which contained five bones (three arm and two shin bones) and some locks of hair, was draped in a Confederate flag. Quantrill was given a military funeral with full honors. A twenty-one-gun salute was provided by a group of reenactors from the 5th Missouri Infantry, C.S.A. After the funeral, Hawkins asked that "anyone who cares to honor this man or any of the men who rode with him to pass by the grave and cast a bit of soil upon the casket" (Leslie 435).

Less than a week later, on October 30, 1992, Quantrill's skull, encased in a child's coffin was buried in his hometown of Dover, Ohio, to much less fanfare than was seen in Higginsville. Less than twenty people looked on as the skull was buried about three feet deep to ensure that the bones buried in 1889 were not disturbed.

Figure 130: Quantrill's grave located in Dover, Ohio

It would take another sixteen years for a marker to be placed at Quantrill's original gravesite in Kentucky, but eventually, on October 25, 2008, a marker was placed on Quantrill's original grave in St. John Catholic Cemetery in Louisville. While the actual number of attendees is not available, this was said to be a well-organized and attended event. Speakers at the service included representatives from Mollie Morehead United Daughters of the Confederacy, several commanders from the Sons of the Confederacy, a representative from the Granite Rose Society and Patrick Marquis, the founder of www.Quantrillsguerrillas.com a source from which information about this service was gathered (quantrillsguerrillas.com).

Figure 131: Quantrill's grave in Louisville, Kentucky, St. John Cemetery. The inscription reads: "In Memory, Col. William Clarke Quantrill, July 31, 1837 - June 6, 1865, Here's a sigh to those who love me and a smile for those who hate and whatever sky's above me. Here a heart for every fate."

Quantrill Reunions

It took some time, but eventually, the stigma of being a member of Quantrill's band transitioned from being something that was not mentioned due to possible legal ramifications, to being something that the men were proud of and more than willing to share with anyone who would ask. Quantrill's men were not ashamed of their time riding with Quantrill, far from it. Most of these men were very proud of their actions during the war and felt, up to their last breath, that they were doing what they were forced to do at the time to protect their families and their property.

In 1898, a small group of Quantrill's men and some of their wives gathered in Blue Springs for a reception held for Quantrill's mother, Caroline, who had come to the area to meet with some of the men who rode with her son. Remember that Caroline did not have a great deal of information about her son's activities, as she had not heard from him since his last letter in 1860. Of course, his name was all over the newspapers during the war, but Mrs. Quantrill wanted to hear the stories from the men who rode with him during his days in Missouri, as well as any that could shed light on the circumstances of his death in 1865.

Frank James and other members of Quantrill's band got the word out, and

QUANTRELL'S MEN TOGETHER

GUERRILLAS OF THE BORDER MEET THIRTY-FIVE YEARS AFTER.

Thirty-Seven of Them Brought Together at the Blue Springs Picnic by Frank James—A Reunion Every Year After This.

Figure 132: Announcement of the first Quantrill Reunion, printed in the Kansas City Star on September 11, 1898

this, first of many, reunions took place in Blue Springs in August of 1898. The *Kansas City Star* reported that thirty-seven members attended that first reunion. It was this smaller gathering that gave Frank James the idea to hold annual reunions beginning the next year. The annual reunions would continue at various locations until 1929 when the last one was held at the Wallace farm in Independence, Missouri. Images from those reunions appear in the next few pages.

The reader should be aware that there is some dispute about which photos were taken in certain years. For example, several sources attribute the image in figure 133, with the trees in the background as being from the 1912 reunion. Another source, www.rulen.com, a website whose content is centered around the history of the Missouri Partisan Rangers, makes a strong argument that it is, instead, the 1898 reunion. The website's logic is that Frank James, who is the ninth man from the left, wearing a brown jacket, looks relatively young. If the image was from the 1912 reunion, James, who passed away in 1915, would have been 70 years old. He looks to be a much younger man in

Figure 133: Quantrill Reunion, 1899? Sources vary on the date of this image; research says that the date is likely between 1899 and 1901

this photo. Much of the confusion is likely caused by the fact that the date on the postcard is 1912, which is the first year that the Williamson Haffner Publishing Company started publishing them. Another source, www.wcqsociety.com dates the image as 1901, which is still consistent with the rulen.com analysis.

After the decision was made to hold the reunions annually, the men organized the "Quantrill Men Survivor's Association" a group that would organize and coordinate locations and activities at the annual gatherings. The reunions would become a significant annual event for Jackson County during the years in which they were held. A "festival" like atmosphere was the norm as the gatherings included political speeches, storytelling, music, dancing and pot-luck picnics organized by the women. According to the *Kansas City World*, at its height, the reunion would draw as many as 3,000 spectators and participants to Jackson County. This turned the reunion into an economic boom to the locations chosen as the reunion sites. Restaurants, hotels, caterers and many other businesses benefited from the mass influx of people into their towns.

In the second year, 1899, the reunion was held at the fairgrounds in Lee's Summit. The *Kansas City Gazette* described the reunion this way:

> The annual reunion of Quantrell's [sic] old command was held yesterday at the Jackson County fair at Lee's Summit. Eighty-one responded to the roll call....
> When the band struck up "Dixie" every head was bared and every throat gave forth the terrible staccato "rebel yell," with which they terrified the unarmed men and boys at Lawrence before they shot them down as they ran or poked the muzzle of their guns into hiding places to kill them like rats in their holes.
> The public sentiment of the east half of Jackson county, twenty miles from here, has not changed so much since then but that Quantrell's [sic] band was the chief attraction of the fair. As the people of that region glory in the exploits of Jesse James so they still glorify the raiders of Lawrence.

It is worth noting that these festivals, often called "encampments" due to their military relationship, were quite common at this time, not just for Quantrill's band, but also for other veteran soldier's groups, both Union and Confederate. Veterans from these groups would often attend encampments for other related groups. For example, many

Confederate veterans would attend the Quantrill reunions. While Quantrill's men welcomed these men at their event, they also began wearing special red ribbons on their lapels to distinguish them as real "Quantrill Men" rather than just regular Confederate veterans. This desire for distinction tells us that, at this time in western Missouri, these men were considered heroes and very proud of their association with Quantrill. History books would eventually paint them in a much less favorable light.

As one might imagine the people of Kansas and particularly those in Lawrence, held a less than favorable view of these reunions. To them, they seemed to celebrate the deeds of men, who, in their minds, were criminals and murderers. A letter penned by a former Union soldier in Kentucky described the event this way:

> *The most extraordinary reunion of any of the men who took part in the attempt to destroy the country because it involved these shriveled up old demons glorifying the days when they murdered prisoners, ravished women, and pillaged towns, with as much delight and seeming honor as any of the brave Confederate soldiers who recognized the rules of war, would speak of their battles and service. (Quantrell's [sic] Cutthroats)*

In 1905, the *Tonganoxie Mirror* described the reunion in this way:

> *Cole Younger, a convicted thief and murderer, was one of the leading spirits of the reunion of Quantrill's cutthroats in Jackson County, Mo., last week. After all, Younger is no worse than the rest of that gang. Those reunions are nothing less than celebrations to perpetuate the memory of horrible crimes. (4)*

Some Kansas residents took their displeasure with these reunions to the next level when, in 1905, they called on Missouri's Governor, Joseph W. Folk, to extradite many of Quantrill's raiders to Kansas to stand trial for murder. This call was made when a lawyer in Kansas realized that the murder indictments, that had been filed against many of the Bushwhackers after the Lawrence Raid in 1863, had never been canceled and thus were still in effect. Missouri Governor Joseph Folk, a southern Democrat, never acknowledged this request and it is doubtful that any type of official request was ever made.

Figure 134: 1911 Quantrill Reunion Photo

Beginning in 1912, the Quantrill reunions would be held at Wallace Grove in Independence. John C. Wallace, a Southern Sympathizer from Independence, owned a 2,000-acre farm which stretched from the Blue River to what is now Mount Washington Cemetery. The Wallace property was heavily wooded and served as a refuge and a hideout for Quantrill and his men during the war. The homestead that Wallace had built, along with several other smaller homes, was destroyed by federal troops after Order No 11 was issued on August 25, 1863.

The Wallace family returned to their home after the war to find the entire farm in ruins. John Wallace was said to have been arrested earlier in the war by Union soldiers and sentenced to hang. He was reportedly rescued by Quantrill and his men on the night of the hanging. John's daughter, Lizzie Wallace, carried on her father's hatred of the Union loyalists and vowed to open the property for the reunions "as long as a Quantrill man still lived" (Kansas City Star).

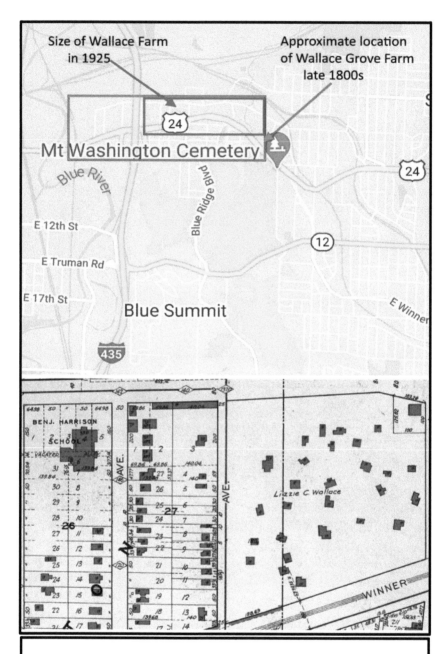

Figure 135: Top: Image shows the approximate location of the Wallace Farm in the mid to late 1800s stretching from the Blue River to Mount Washington Cemetery. Bottom: Kansas City Atlas map showing the Lizzie Wallace Farm in 1925

One of the traditions of reunions at the Wallace farm was to gather on the front porch with a picture of Quantrill placed prominently in the photo. The Quantrill photo spent the rest of the year proudly displayed in the Wallace home. This tradition can be seen in all the reunion photos taken after 1911.

Over time the attendance of the reunions began to dwindle, for the simple reason that the men who had ridden with Quantrill were old and many were now dead or dying. It is estimated that for the first 18 years of the reunion, approximately thirty to thirty-five actual raiders attended. After 1917, the number never exceeded fifteen and after 1922, it was never above single digits. The last five years only saw three Bushwhackers attending.

Figure 136: 1920 Quantrill Reunion at Wallace Farm

Warren Welch, who was elected "captain" at the first reunion, continued to serve as the unofficial historian until he died in 1920. In this role, Welch maintained the books for the reunion, which included the list of members. This list contained the names and contact information for all the raiders and was used to send out invitations each year with details about the reunions. Unfortunately, when Welch died in 1920, nobody could find the book with the names in it, as Welch had always kept it hidden. This meant that going forward, the men would have to find out about the reunion through word of mouth, as they would no longer receive an invitation. This, along with the age of the Bushwhackers, contributed to the smaller attendance figures (Hulbert).

It was in 1922 that future President Harry S. Truman started his political career by speaking at the Quantrill Reunion, held at the Wallace Grove farm. At the time, Truman was campaigning for Eastern Judge of Jackson County. Truman, who was proud of his southern heritage, would later claim to have attended the Quantrill reunion multiple times over the years. He made his feeling on Quantrill and his men clear when he said:

Quantrill and his men were no more bandits than the men on the other side. I've been to reunions of Quantrill's men two or three times. All they were trying to do was protect the property on the Missouri side of the line" (Lacy).

Figure 137: President Harry S. Truman, Independence resident. Truman claimed to have attended two or three Quantrill Reunions

Baltimore's *The Evening Sun* in their September 3, 1931 edition, summed up the era of the Quantrill Reunion in this way:

Now the last roll has been called, and Quantrill's men have disappeared into the shadows. They gave violence to an age that demanded violence, yet most of them lived to prove that they loved peace more than war, sobriety and honesty more than crime. (25)

Conclusion

When I first began working on this project, I was very excited to have found, in the Raid of Olathe, a topic that had not been fully covered. As a Civil War enthusiast and Olathe resident, I felt that a work on the topic would contribute to the store of historical knowledge about my hometown. My excitement for the topic never waned, rather, it intensified and broadened to include a much larger view of the era that went well beyond the Olathe Raid.

Throughout my research, I spoke with many people across the Missouri/Kansas border on the topic. It became clear to me that significant causes and events of the Border War era were things that current residents knew very little about. Growing up in Harrisonville, I don't remember being taught any specifics about the Border War; why it happened or how it impacted my hometown. We learned about the Lawrence Raid, but that was about the extent of our Border War education. We learned that the evil and bloodthirsty guerrillas led by Quantrill murdered many people in Lawrence and then burned down the entire town.

We were taught very little about what led to that event, nor of the events that had occurred on the Missouri side of the border. I feel confident that on the Kansas side, students were taught with much the same lens. In Harrisonville specifically, I don't remember learning anything about Order Number 11. I knew there was an engraved marker telling about it in front of the courthouse, but I had never bothered to read the message on the plaque. Generations have grown up thinking that the raid on Lawrence is the whole reason for the historic tension between Missouri and Kansas. This project has shown me that there are many more layers to the Missouri/Kansas conflict.

Blame should not be pointed at local history teachers for the omission of the Border War details in their classrooms. To be fair, the raid on Lawrence is one of the few things mentioned in the nationally printed history textbooks used in most schools. These textbooks spend their time on Gettysburg, Antietam, Shiloh and Appomattox. They don't seem to have room for what was happening in the west. The fighting in Missouri and Kansas did not involve large armies in pitched battles where thousands of men were dying and was thus not worth the space in our textbooks.

The turmoil on the Missouri/Kansas border between 1854 and the end of the Civil War in 1865 was a microcosm of the troubles facing the entire country at the time. The country's issues were being replicated on the border but happening on a much smaller scale. The Bleeding Kansas era was marked by forces from opposite sides invading the Kansas Territory attempting to ensure that Kansas was admitted to the United States as either a slave or a free-state. For some men, slavery was a central issue. Kansans like John Brown, James Montgomery and Doc Jennison were ardent abolitionists who began their careers entirely focused on the goal of making sure that the spread of slavery was stopped, and the practice was not allowed in the new Kansas Territory.

On the Missouri side, there were those men who were specifically fighting to keep slavery, but the reality is that most Missourians were not slave owners. Those that were, likely owned only one or two slaves. Most of these men were likely farmers who identified with the ideals of the Southern way of life. The primary motive that led Missourians and other Southerners to push for Kansas to be a slave state was that if the industrial north gained control of the government, the agricultural south would eventually be squeezed out of political decision making. If the north gained control, the southern "way of life" might be eliminated. This agricultural "way of life" was coupled very tightly with the institution of slavery in the public mindset.

The battle over the status of slavery in the state of Kansas was largely pitched on Kansas soil, with its residents bearing the brunt of the pain. This pain to Kansans came in the form of supplies being intercepted on their way into the state, as well as the practice of terrorizing Free-Staters into not voting or even forcing them out of the state. The expulsion of those persons with opposite slavery viewpoints was a tactic used by both sides from 1855 through 1858. In the early years of that period, the pro-slavery advocates were in control of the government and thus had the force of the law on their side. By 1859 the tide had turned, and the free-state men had taken over the government. These free-staters, now with the force of the government behind them, were led by men such as Lane and Jennison who would use the power afforded them by the government to do what they could to remove all pro-slavery settlers from the state of Kansas.

The Bleeding Kansas era, which generally is considered to have lasted from 1854-1859, while certainly a difficult time for Kansas settlers, was not an inordinately "bloody era". Historians estimate that only about 55 persons on both sides of the slavery issue were killed during the Bleeding Kansas years (African). There was significant property theft and damage during this time frame, but the death toll was relatively low. The term "Bleeding Kansas" is a bit misleading in that regard.

The death and destruction would be ramped up significantly with the onset of the of the U.S. Civil War. Kansas troops, primarily under Lane and Jennison, invaded Missouri to make Missourians, pro and anti-slavery alike, pay for what Missourians had done during the Bleeding Kansas era. Numbers are difficult to come by in terms of fatalities and overall destruction inflicted on Missouri residents during the winter of 1861-1862 alone, but it is certain that the body count in the wake of these Jayhawker raids, surpassed the total body count of the entire Bleeding Kansas era. It was these raids by Kansans into Missouri, and the trail of destruction the Jayhawkers left behind that seems to be largely forgotten by mainstream history textbooks. This omission means that students are not learning about the "other" side of the Border War. Knowledge of these facts is limited to those whose interest in the topic has led them to study the history of the era at a much deeper level.

It is the invasions by Jayhawk leaders that led to the creation of guerrilla groups, such as the one led by William Quantrill. These Bushwhackers were groups of men who initially were only looking to try and help protect Missouri residents and their property from the actions of the Jayhawkers. The Jayhawkers were little more than large bands of organized and legitimized thieves, acting in the name of the Federal Government. Over time, the same temptations that took many of the Jayhawkers down a more criminal route would also claim a large percentage of the Missouri Bushwhackers.

Our modern view of Civil War history has painted the Union side of the war as highly moral citizens with the sole purpose of ending slavery. This is simply not true. While there were Northerners, such as the Abolitionists, who fervently believed in the freeing of the slaves, it should be noted that this goal was never listed by the U.S. Government as an official reason for the war. On July 25, 1861, the U.S. Congress passed the Crittendon-Johnson Resolution which declared that the "war was being waged for the reunion of the states and not to interfere with slavery." In fact, for the first two years of the war, it was illegal for federal soldiers to interfere with the practice of slavery in any state. It wasn't until the Emancipation Proclamation issued by President Lincoln on January 1st, 1863, that slavery was outlawed, with exceptions. The most notable exception is that the slavery was only outlawed in the states that had seceded from the Union. Lincoln's Emancipation Proclamation did "NOT" free slaves in the border states of Missouri, Kentucky, Maryland, West Virginia or Delaware. In fact, slavery in Missouri was not abolished for two more years when in January of 1865, a state convention abolished slavery in the state.

Also remember that, the initial version of the Topeka Constitution, created by the non-recognized Free-State Legislature in 1855, did outlaw slavery in the state, but also excluded "Negroes and Mulattoes" from living in the new state. This sentiment was common throughout the northern states. These "highly moral" people fall short in the prism of today's world view with their attitude of "we support the freeing of the slaves, as long as they don't live near us". This belief would continue for many years after the close of the Civil War and most Americans would admit that, sadly, this sentiment still exists today.

The raid of Olathe was one of several raids into Kansas, perpetrated by the Bushwhackers, in response to some real or perceived transgression perpetrated by the Kansas Jayhawkers or the Union Army. As mentioned earlier, the story of the Border War, including the Bleeding Kansas era, was one of each side constantly seeking revenge for an action by the other. The Olathe Raid was in direct response to the execution of Perry Hoy. The Lawrence raid was said to be, in part, in response to the purposeful collapse of the Kansas City women's prison. Lane and Jennison's raids into Missouri in 1861, were meant to exact revenge for past actions by Missourians who had entered Kansas to illegally vote in state elections. The cycle of revenge continued through the end of the Civil War.

When asked by a *St. Louis Post-Dispatch* reporter how he justified killing unarmed men during the Lawrence Raid, J.A. Workman, a Quantrill man attending the 1902 reunion, responded with this comment:

Young man, I'm afraid you would never make a good soldier. Those Kansas Redlegs came over here and laid waste to our homes. What would you think of a man or party of men who would come to your home and take your wife and young baby out and lay them on a mattress in the snow a foot deep and then burn down your house?

Those things were done here. In some of our counties, we didn't have seven houses left standing. Naturally, the men of our families were enraged. We couldn't stay at home; we would have been shot. We went out and shot; we went after the men who had done those devilish deeds" (8/24/1902).

Workman would go on to explain the action of Quantrill and his men during the war by saying, "What we did, we did. It was war, and in war, men go forth and kill men." It is likely that when asked, men on both sides would use the same logic to defend actions that, when viewed from a historical perspective, appear to be criminal and often horrific. Confederate General Patrick Cleburne's statement would prove prophetic when during the war he said:

Surrender means that the history of this heroic struggle will be written by the enemy; that our youth will be trained by Northern school teachers; will learn from Northern school books their version of the War; will be impressed by all the influences of history and education to regard our gallant dead as traitors, and our maimed veterans as fit subjects for derision. (Peterson 434)

Quantrill's actions at Olathe and most of his other raids into Kansas, or upon Union-controlled garrisons, paint a picture of a commander of an efficient military unit who efficiently went about the work of achieving their objectives. It isn't until we layer in the atrocities committed in the raid on Lawrence that we begin to think of Quantrill and his men as bloodthirsty murderers. Prior to Lawrence, the only men killed in Quantrill's raids were those who directly defied orders or were thought to have perpetrated some other act for which they needed to be held accountable. Remember that is also around the time of the Olathe Raid, that the Union Army began its' policy of "no quarter" for any prisoner who was thought to have participated in bushwhacker raids.

This does not mean that Quantrill and his men, or other guerrilla groups like his, didn't commit murder. They did. They were soldiers fighting for a cause and the method they employed was hit and run guerrilla tactics, meant to inflict damage on enemy military units. This fighting often resulted in death on both sides. The distinction here is between regular military actions and Bushwhacker raids on towns such as Olathe and Lawrence, or on the Missouri side; Jayhawker raids on Osceola or Dayton. During Quantrill's raid of Lawrence, his habit of maintaining military decorum seemed to have been forgotten during a murderous morning that would change the historical perspective of Quantrill and his men forever.

None of the men featured in this book were angels. Once the facts are known, it becomes difficult for either side to claim the moral high ground. The reality is that men on both sides committed acts that would be considered criminal back then just as they would today. The temptation to use the war as an opportunity to attain personal wealth or revenge proved to be too much for many of the men on both sides of the conflict to resist. It is also unfair to paint these men entirely as common criminals. The men fighting in the Border War felt that they were doing what they had to do to protect their property, or to be compensated for what had been taken from them by the other side. These men, particularly on the Missouri side, felt that the guerrilla life was the only choice available to them, due to the consistent mismanagement of the Border War region by the Federal Government during the Civil War years.

In today's politically charged environment, we have reduced the Civil War to the idea that anyone fighting for the Confederacy was fighting for slavery and anyone fighting for the Union was fighting against the reprehensible institution. This view is simply not accurate. The reality is that during the Civil War, the situation was not so clear cut. Was slavery an issue in the Civil War? Absolutely. Was it the main issue for the conflict? Maybe for some, but certainly not for all. This statement in no way diminishes the dark and embarrassing time in U.S. history when our ancestors thought that enslaving other human beings was an acceptable practice. However, blaming just the Southern states or the Confederacy for the institution of slavery is to ignore historical facts and give everyone who supported the Union a free pass on the many years where slavery was supported in those states.

When judging the Jayhawkers and Bushwhackers from a historical perspective, it is critical to empathize with these men and the situation in which they found themselves. It's easy to look back now on actions taken by men on both sides of the conflict and condemn them for actions that today seem reprehensible. It is only when we step into their shoes that we can begin to understand what they were going through, which led them to the actions for which they are now judged.

Bibliography

Adair, Donna. "Quantrill's Raid on Olathe." *EzineArticles*, 7 Aug. 2011, .https://ezinearticles.com/?Quantrills-Raid-on-Olathe,-Kansas,-September-6,-1862&id=6478781.

"Africans in American: Bleeding Kansas." *www.pbs.org/wgbh*, PBS, www.pbs.org/wgbh/aia/part4/4p2952.html.

Anderson, Ethan. "Confederate Memorialization int he Free-State." *www.kansasmemory.org*, Kansas State Historical Society, 10 Sept. 2020, www.kansasmemory.org/blog/post/326605106. Accessed 21 Oct. 2020.

Anderson, JR. "Guerilla Raids Important Facet During Civil War." *Great Bend Tribune* [Great Bend, Kansas], 19 Dec. 1960, p. 3.

Anderson, JR. "Quantrill's Raiders a Motley Group." *Great Bend Tribune* [Great Bend, Kansas], 20 Dec. 1960, p. 10.

"A Rebel Reunion," 17 May 1888, Grand Army Advocate; "Quantrell's Cutthroats," 17 May 1888, Grand Army Advocate.

Atchison, David R. "David R. Atchison Speech to Proslavery Forces." *Kansas Memory*, Kansas State Historical Society, 21 May 1856, www.kansasmemory.org/item/90822/text.

Banks, James A. *United States: Adventures in Time and Place*. New York, NY, McGraw-Hill School Division, 1999.

"Battle of Albany Monument." *Find a Grave*, Find A Grave, www.findagrave.com/memorial/65585966/battleof-albany_monument.

"Battle of Hickory Point Kansas." *https://www.legendsofamerica.com*, www.legendsofamerica.com/ks-hickorypointbattle/.

"Bill Anderson Killed." *Lawrence Tribune* [Lawrence, Kansas], 3 Nov. 1864 Beilein, Joseph M., Jr., editor. *William Gregg's Civil War: The Bat tle to Shape the History of Guerrilla Warfare*. Atlanta, GA, Univer sity of Georgia Press, 2019.

Blackmar, Frank W. *Kansas, A Cyclopedia of State History, Embracing Events, Institutions, Industries, Counties, Cities, Towns, Prominent Persons etc.* Vol. 1, Chicago, Standard Publishing Company, 1912. 2 vols.

Blair, Ed. *History of Johnson County*. Lawrence Kansas, Stand Publishing Company, 1915.

"Bleeding Kansas." *www.Khanacademy.org*, Khan Academy, www.khanacademy.org/humanities/us-history/civil-war-era/sectional-tension-1850s/a/bleeding-kansas.

"Border Counties." *Olathe Mirror* [Olathe], 20 Mar. 1862, p. 2.

Bridgman, Edward. "Letter from Edward Bridgman." *www.PBS.org*, PBS, 25 May 1856, www.pbs.org/wgbh/aia/part4/4h2953t.html.

Breihan, Carl W. *Quantrill and his Civil War Guerrillas*. New York, NY, Promontory Press, 1959.

Brophy, Pr. *Bushwhackers of the Border*. Nevada, Missouri, Vernon County Historical Society, 1980.

Brownlee, Richard S. *Gray Ghosts of the Confederacy: Guerrilla Warfare in the West*. Baton Rouge, LA, Louisiana State University Press, 1958.

Castel, Albert. William Clarke Quantrill; His Life and Times. University of Oklahoma Press, 1962.

"Charles R. Jennison Obituary." *The Kansas Prohibitionist* [Columbus, Kansas], 25 June 1884, p. 5.

"Col. C. R. Jennison." *Leavenworth Times* [Leavenworth, Kansas], 14 Dec. 1871, p. 2.

Connelley, William E. *A Standard History of Kansas and Kansans*. Vol. 1, Chicago, Lewis Publishing Company, 1919.

Connelley, William E. *Quantrill and Border Wars*. Torch Press Publishers, 1910.

Cutler, William G. *History of the State of Kansas*, A.T. Andreas, (1883), "Territorial History, Part 8"

Davenport Democrat [Davenport]. 27 Aug. 1856.

"Doings of the Kansas Legislature." *Anti Slavery Bugle* [Lisbon, Ohio], 4 Aug. 1855, p. 1.

Drouin, Jeremy. "Of Raiders and Reunions: A KC Q Answered." *The Kansas City Public Library*, KCLibrary.org, 2 July 2019, www.kclibrary.org/blog/raiders-and-reunions-kc-q-answered. Accessed 27 Apr. 2020.

Drouin, Jeremy. "The Quantrill name, legacy in Kansas City: We answer a 'Border War' KCQ." *KansasCity.com*, Kansas City Public Library, 21 June 2019, www.kansascity.com/news/ your-kcq/article231691193.html.

Dyer, Robert L. *Jesse James and the Civil War in Missouri*. Columbia, U of Missouri Press, 1994.

"Early History of Olathe, Kansas." *Northwood Trails Newsletter*.

Edmonds, George. *Facts and Falsehoods Concerning the War on the South 1861-1865*. A.R. Taylor and Company, 1904.

Edwards, John N. *Noted Guerrillas or the Warfare of the Border: Being a History of the Lives and Adventures of Quantrell, Bill Anderson and Numerous Other Well-Known Guerrillas of the West*. St. Louis, MO, Bryan, Brand, 1877.

Edwards, Nick. *Hidden in Plain Site: Aubry, Johnson County, Kansas 1858-1888.*

Erwin, James W. Guerrillas in Civil War Missouri. Charleston, SC, History Press, 2012.

Etchesen, Nicole. "Jennison's Jayhawkers." *New York Times* [New York], 26 Apr. 2016.

Evening Sun [Baltimore, Maryland]. 3 Sept. 1931.

"Everything Ablaze on the Western Missouri Border: Ewing's General Order Number 11." *The New Sante Fe Trailer*, 24 Aug. 2017, www.newsantafetrailer.blogspot.com/2017/08/tensions-ablaze-on-missouri-border.html. Accessed 28 July 2020.

"Fate of Two Who Loved the Daring Guerrilla and Who Maintained That History Had Dealt Unjustly with Him." *St. Louis Post-Dispatch* [St. Louis, Missouri], 9 Dec. 1900, p. 49.

"The First Kansas Cavalry Takes Independence - Negroes and Properties of Rebels Confiscated." *White Cloud Kansas Chief* [White Cloud, Kansas], 21 Nov. 1861.

Fry, Alice L. *Following the Fifth Kansas Cavalry: The Letters*. Lebanon, Missouri, The Blue and Gray Book Shoppe, 1998.

"General Jim Lane." *The Daily Argus* [Rock Island, Illinois], 12 June 1856, p. 2.

Gilmore, Donald L. "The Kansas Red Legs: The Dark Underbelly of the Civil War in Missouri." Https://www.academia.edu. Manuscript.

Gilmore, Donald L. *Civil War on the Missouri-Kansas Border*. Gretna, LA, Pelican Publishing Co, 2006.

Goodrich Bisel, Debra. *The Civil War in Kansas: Ten Years of Turmoil*. History Press, 2012.

Goodrich, Thomas. *Black Flag, Guerrilla Warfare on the Western Border, 1861-1865*. Indiana University Press, 1995.

Goodrich, Thomas. *War to the Knife: Bleeding Kansas, 1854-1861*. Mechanicsburg, PA, Stackpole Books, 1998.

Gregg, Oliver H. "History of Johnson County Kansas." *jocohistory.org*, www.jocohistory.org/digital/collection/atlas/id/8/rec/1.

"Guerrillas in Kansas." *Chicago Tribune* [Chicago Illinois], 13 Sept. 1862, p. 2.

Hale, Donald R. "Another Chapter in the Quantrill's Story." *Kansas City Times* [Kansas City], 13 Apr. 1973.

Hall, Jesse A., and Leroy T. Hand. *History of Leavenworth County Kansas.* Topeka, KS, Historical Publishing Company, 1921.

Hermon, Gregory. "The Night Olathe Almost Died." *In Old Johnson County*, vol. 1, 1944.

Hicks, John Edward. "Bloody Quantrill: A Researcher's Unbiased Look." *Kansas City Times* [Kansas City], 6 Apr. 1963, p. 42.

Historic Olathe: The comprehensive Historic Preservation Plan for the city of Olathe, Kansas. Olathe, Kansas, Rosin Preservation & Draw Architecture + Urban Design, Aug. 2013.

History Channel Editors. "Bleeding Kansas." *www.History.com*, History Channel, 19 Oct. 2018, www.history.com/topics/19th-century/bleeding-kansas , www.history.com.

Hulbert, Matthew Christopher. *The Ghosts of Guerrilla Memory: How Civil War Bushwhackers Became Gunslingers in the American West.* U of Georgia Press, 2016. UnCivil War Series.

Hulbert, Matthew Christopher. "The Rise and Fall of Edwin Terrill, Guerrilla Hunter, USA." *Ohio Valley History*, vol. 18, Number 3, pp. 42-61.

"Immigration and Early Settlement." *https://territorialkansasonline .ku.edu.*territorialkansasonline.ku.edu/index.php?SCREEN= immigration &option=more.

"Interesting News from Kansas." *NY Daily Herald* [New York, New York], 9 Jan. 1856, p. 2.

"James Henry Lane." Wikipedia, Wikimedia Foundation, 10 June 2020, https://en.wikipedia.org/wiki/James_Henry_Lane_(Union_general)

James Henry Lane: Grim Chieftain." *Decade of Decision 1855-1865.* Kansas City, KC Life Company, 1960.

"Jim Lane's Tactics." *Ashtabula Weekly Telegraph* [Ashtabula, OH], 1 9 Oct. 1861.

John, Blum M. *The National Experience: A History of the United States.* New York, NY, Harcourt, Brace & World, 1963.

Kamberg, Mary-Lane. "Band of Brothers Broken." *TrueWestMagazine.com*, 1 June 2005,   truewestmagazine.com/ band -of-brothers-broken/.

"Kansas invaded! Olathe Sacked! Newspaper destroyed! Quantrill at work!" *Western Home Journal* [Lawrence, Kansas], 18th ed., 11 Sept. 1862, p. 2.

"The Kansas Senators." *Memphis Daily Argus* [Memphis, TN], 9 Apr. 1861, p. 2.

Kemp, Pauline E. "Where Truman's Campaign Trail Began." *Kansas City Times* [Kansas City, Missouri], 7 May 1970, p. 75.

Lacy, Clint E. "Missouri's Confederate Ties." *Southeast Missourian* [Cape Girardeau, Missouri], 31 Oct. 2004.

"Lecompton - Capitol of Kansas Territory." *Legends of America*, legendsofkansas.com/lecompton-kansas/.

Leslie, Edward E. "The Devil Knows How to Ride". Da Capo Press, 1996 "Lest we Forget." *http://www.quantrillsguerrillas.com*, www.quantrillsguerrillas.com/en/articles/231-lest-we-forget.html.

"Letter from Edward Bridgman." *PBS.org*, PBS, www.pbs.org/wgbh/aia/part4/4h2953t.html .

Litteer, Loren K. *"Bleeding Kansas" The Border War in Douglas and Adjacent Counties*. Baldwin Kansas, Champion Publishing, 2002.

McCorkle, John, and O.S. Barton. *Three Years with Quantrill, A True Story Told by his Scout:* Armstrong Herald Print, 1914.

McCoy, Max. *I, Quantrill*. Signet, 2008.

McGregor, Andrew. "The Terrible Tale of Bloody Bill Anderson: Rebellion and Revenge on the Missouri Frontier." *Aberfoyle International Security*, 3 Apr. 2019, www.aberfoylesecurity.com/?tag=george-todd.

"The Memorial Stone Dedication Which Took 143 years." *Quantrill's guerrillas*, quantrillsguerrillas.com.

Miller, George, b. 1834. Missouri's Memorable Decade, 1860-1870: An Historical Sketch, Personal, Political, Religious. Columbia, Mo.: Press of E. W. Stephens, 1898.

Milhoan, JH. "When Quantrill Raided OlatheHttp://genealogytrails.com/kan/johnson/history/johnsonhistory13.html Manuscript.

The Missouri Partisan Ranger. www.rulen.com/partisan/1912.htm.

Morris, Colin. *Panic Spreads in Johnson County as a Nation divides: a look back at forgotten Tuscarora Lake*. Chapman Center for Urban Studies, 2016.

Morrison, Francis R. "Squiresville and the Civil War." *Sharing Memories*, pp. 35-40.

"Official report of General Burris." *The Smokey Hill and Republican Union* [Junction City, Kansas], 4 Oct. 1862.

"Olathe KS search results." *digital.lib.ku.edu*, Kansas University, digital.lib.ku.edu/islandora/search/olathe%20ks?type=edismax&cp =ku-sanborn%3Aroot.

Olsen, Kevin G.W. *Frontier Manhattan: Yankee Settlement to Kansas Town, 1854-1894*. University Press of Kansas, 2012.

"Quantrill's Men Reunion, Independence, Mo." *Ozarkscivilwar.org*, Springfield-Greene County Library System, ozarkscivilwar.org /photographs/quantrills-men-reunion/.

Parsons, Samuel, Jr. "The evolution of a city square." *Scribner's Magazine*, vol. XII, July 1892, p. 107.

Peterson, Paul. "Approximate Number of Missouri Homes burned by J ayhawkers & Red-Legs." *Quantrillsguerrillas.com*, www.quantrill sguerrillas.com/en/articles/88-approximate-number-of-missouri-ho mes-burned-by-jayhawkers-redlegs-article.html.

Peterson, Paul R. *Quantrill of Missouri: The Making of a Guerrilla Wa rrior*. Nashville, TN, Cumberland House Publishing, 2003.

"Quantrill." *Olathe, "the city beautiful centennial 1857-1957*.

"Quantrill's Prisoner." *Olathe: Facts Photos Letters and Legends*, pp. 25-26.

"Quantrill's Raids." *www.Kansas State Historical Society.org*, Kansas Historical Society, July 2013, **Error! Hyperlink reference not valid.**.

Rafiner, Tom A. *Cinders and Silence: A Chronicle of Missouri's Burnt District 1854-1870*. Harrisonville, MO, Burnt District Press, 2013.

"Rebel's remains finally find rest." *Springfield News Leader* [Springfield, Missouri], 25 Oct. 1992, p. 14.

Reiber, Beth. "It wasn't called Bleeding Kansas for nothing." *www.explorelawrence.com*, Lawrence Convention & Visitors Bureau, 26 July 2018, unmistakablylawrence.com/history-heritage/bleeding-kansas/.

Roe, Jason. "Evacuation Day." *KCHistory.org*, Kansas City Library,w ww.kchistory.org/seek-kansas-city-history/evacuation-day.

Love, Robertus. "Rough Rider Quantrill as His Men Knew Him." *St. Louis Post-Dispatch* [St. Louis, Missouri], 24 Aug. 1902, p. 13.

Schultz, Duane. *Quantrill's War: The Life and Times of William Clark e Quantrill*. New York, NY, St. Martin's Griffin, 1997.

Schwenk, Sarah F., et al. *The Cultural Resources of Blue Springs, Missouri*. National Park Service, Aug. 1986.

Soodalter, Ronald. "THE 1861 JAYHAWKER RAID IN OSCEOLA." *www.missourilife.com*, Missouri Life Magazine, 6 Aug. 2019, missourilife.com/the-1861-jayhawker-raid-in-osceola/.

Speer, John. "The Burning of Osceola, MO, by Lane and the Quantrill Massacre Contrasted." 1899. *Quantrill: The first American Terrori st*, Kansas State Historical Society, 2002, pp. 68- 75.

St. Louis Post-Dispatch [St. Louis, Missouri]. 24 Aug. 1902.

Thavis, L. W. "Quantrel's Raid of Olathe." *Olathe News-Herald* [Olathe Kansas], 15 Jan. 1897, p. 1.

Tabor, Chris. *In the Eye of the Storm: Bates County and the First Year of the Civil War, 1861.* Butler, Missouri, Bates County Historical Society, 1999.

"The Town of Olathe Sacked." *The Oskaloosa Independent* [Oskaloosa Kansas], 13 Sept. 1862.

"They Glory in Their Shame. "*Kansas City Gazette* [Kansas City], 14 Sept. 1899, p. 1.

Titterington, Dick. "http://www.thecivilwarmuse.com/." *http://www.th ecivilwarmuse.com/*, Grawader Enterprises, 2009, www.thecivilwa rmuse.com/.

Tonganoxie Mirror [Tonganoxie, Kansas], 31 Aug. 1905, p. 4.

Townsend, Robert S. *Decade of Decision 1855-1865*. Kansas City, KC Life Company, 1960.

United States, Congress, House. *Report of the Special Committee Appointed to Investigate the Troubles in Kansas.* http://www.wvculture.org/history/jbexhibit/housecommittee.html 1856. Web. 21 Oct.2020.

Ward, Allen T. "Allen T Ward Correspondence." 27 Oct. 1861. Kansas Memory, Kansas State Archives, Topeka, Allen T. Ward Coll. #528, Box 1 Folders 23 - 24. Letter.

Weekly Southern Democrat [Parkville, MO]. 22 Mar. 1855.

Wikipedia Contributors. "James Henry Lane (Union General)." *Wikipe dia.com*, en.wikipedia.org/wiki/James Henry Lane Union General.

"William Quantrill Receipt." *Kansas Memory*, KANSAS STATE HISTORICAL SOCIETY.org, www.Kansas State Historical Society.org/km/items/view/218802.

"William Quantrill – Renegade Leader of the Missouri Border War." *https://www.legendsofamerica.com*, Legends of America, www.legendsofamerica.com/mo-quantrill/.

Wilcox, Pearl. *Jackson County Pioneers*. Independence, Independence Press, 1975.

Wood, Larry. *Call Me Charlie: the story of a Quantrill Raider;* 2016.

Index

About the Author

Jonathan Jones was born and raised in Harrisonville, Missouri. He graduated from Missouri State University with a BS in Business Education and from Park University, where he earned an MBA in International Business. Jones spent ten years as a teacher and coach in Missouri Schools before moving into the business world where he would spend the next 20+ years working as an Enterprise Architect for IAT Insurance Group. Jones is a lifelong history buff and spends much of his spare time researching history, both in his local area as well as traveling to visit historic sites around the world. Jones and his wife of 30 plus years, Jill, have three grown children, Zac, Lexi and Nikai and currently reside in Olathe, Kansas. More information on Jones' work can be found at www.JonathanJonesAuthor.com .

CPSIA information can be obtained
at www.ICGtesting.com
Printed in the USA
BVHW090808030321
601532BV00003B/13